BELIEF AND DISBELIEF

IN

AMERICAN LITERATURE

FRANK L. WEIL
INSTITUTE FOR
STUDIES IN
RELIGION AND
THE HUMANITIES

HOWARD MUMFORD JONES

BELIEF AND DISBELIEF
IN
AMERICAN LITERATURE

CHICAGO & LONDON

THE UNIVERSITY OF CHICAGO PRESS

Library of Congress Catalog Card Number: 67-25521

THE UNIVERSITY OF CHICAGO PRESS, CHICAGO & LONDON
The University of Toronto Press, Toronto 5, Canada

To

JEROME HAMILTON BUCKLEY
student of literature and belief

PREFACE

I have kept the text of these lectures in the form in which they were delivered except for the correcting of a few obvious errors and the addition of a few footnotes. The reader has, it seems to me, the right to share with the audience the original impact of the lecturer's presentation, whatever the faults and virtues of that presentation might be. Since the six addresses were delivered with varying intervals of time between any two of them, each is an autonomous discourse, a fact that creates a mild repetitiveness in a few allusions but not, I trust, anything that will disturb the thoughtful reader. The little "Postlude" at the end of the volume sums up the drift of my analyses as I see it.

I express my thanks for the friendly interest of the audiences that heard me, and to the many Cincinnatians who made the occasion of these discourses memorable by their warm hospitality. Especially must I express my deep gratitude for the patient and affectionate interest of Professor Samuel Sandmel, Chairman of the Frank L. Weil Institute, for his tireless care for the lectures and the lecturer.

I acknowledge with thanks the permission of Harper & Row, publishers of Mark Twain, to quote from various works by or about that author; and of Holt, Rinehart and Winston, for permission to quote from writings of Robert Frost:

CONTENTS

CONTENTS

✦ I ✦

TOM PAINE AND REPUBLICAN RELIGION

I

THESE DISCUSSIONS of the relation between belief and literature in the United States find two lions waiting at the gate: the
meaning of "belief" and the meaning of "literature." I am not
going to define literature, contenting myself with selecting from
the canon of American literary classics six or eight representative writers whose work was done between 1775 and the present
decade. I shall define "belief" no farther than to say that in
American terms it means the acceptance of the idea that there is
a God, that He has some regard for His universe, and that the
values of human life and human personality in some sense have
supernatural sanctions.

Both of these notions have important local limitations. In
America belief and disbelief usually imply the acceptance or re-
jection of a God revealed in some great phase of the Judaeo-
Christian tradition. We have Muslims, Buddhists, Taoists, and
varieties of other theistic faiths among us, but most Americans
mean by "belief" the relation of the individual soul to God in
the Western sense of deity. Moreover, the three great branches of
our tradition are, in order of development, Judaism, Catholicism,
and Protestantism, but the influence of these upon the United
States has been in an order historically reversed, the Protestants

1

coming first, the Catholics second, and the Jews last. There were Jews and Catholics in the colonies from very early times, and Catholicism and Judaism have of late exerted important cultural influences. But from 1607 virtually into our own times the American tradition has been a Protestant tradition. Indeed, there are those who argue that Protestantism is the essential American way or that the American way developed out of Protestantism.

In the *Yearbook of American Churches* for 1965 one finds 253 separate religious bodies reporting to this annual compilation. Church members in 1963 numbered almost seventy million Protestants, almost forty-five million Catholics, and something more than six and one-half million Jews. Professor William Warren Sweet, the historian of American religious life, says that the religious bodies in this country number more than 300, but I doubt that his figure would alter the proportion among the three leading faiths. There is, of course, no necessary connection between the number of sects and their cultural influence and none between the size of their membership and their intellectual importance. It is also true that in this century Catholics and Jews are increasingly influential in shaping American culture. But though I think we are working in religion toward a richer cultural pluralism, the figures seem to show that the Protestant tradition is still dominant. Our literary classics, moreover, have been written either by Protestants, as in the case of Longfellow, or by authors reared in some branch of the Protestant faith and later departing from it, as in the case of Whitman. Standard American literary classics are therefore so overwhelmingly Protestant in tone that I shall seem to be unfair to Catholic and Jewish writers, but the difficulty is inherent in the topic and not of my creating.

Another general observation seems necessary. We have had countless books and essays, articles and sermons on topics like the Bible in America, the influence of the Bible on American literature, religion as a theme in poetry, the religious novel in the United States, and so on, and these are often valuable. But we must distinguish between information about religion, and genuine religious belief, just as we must distinguish between moral intention and artistic success. Many novels on religious themes have been best-sellers, but most of them are negligible as literature. Most religious poetry—hymns, religious anecdotes, hortatory verses, and the like—is second-rate writing. The United States in the nineteenth century produced two unique and influential Bibles—the *Book of Mormon* and *Science and Health with a Key to the Scriptures*, but neither of them is a literary classic. In fact, American literature has never produced a great religious book in the sense that the *Divine Comedy* is a great Catholic masterpiece, *Paradise Lost* a great Protestant masterpiece, and the Book of Job a great Jewish masterpiece. We have, of course, produced religious classics of the second rank; for example, the *Journal* of John Woolman. But literary values frequently move in one direction, religious values in another, and we must continually keep in mind that our inquiry is not whether religious belief or the lack of it has produced American literature, but what a reading of some representative American literary classics reveals about the religious faith or lack of faith of those who wrote them.

II

These preliminary cautions out of the way, I turn briefly to the colonial period. The stretch of time between 1607, when Jamestown was founded, to 1789, when the Federal Constitution was adopted, presents one of the most amazing reversals of value among educated men in all American history. Discoverers, explorers, and settlers in the beginning universally accepted a Christian God, a providential ordering of events, the immortality of the soul, and the doctrines of individual salvation or damnation. In 1789, however, there was a general drift of opinion among American leaders toward deism or to a modification of Christian theology that I can only call Christian deism. Representatives of this tendency are such figures as Washington, Franklin, Jefferson, and Thomas Paine. When Jamestown was founded, it was axiomatic that every nation-state, and therefore every colony, should have some sort of established church. Thus the Rev. John Cotton wrote:

It is better that the commonwealth be fashioned to the setting forth of God's house, which is his church: than to accommodate the church frame to the civill state. Democracy, I do not conceyve that ever God did ordeyne as a fitt government eyther for church or commonwealth.

Cotton died in 1652. As late as 1775 nine of the thirteen original states still maintained an official church establishment, and in the other four, religious toleration was limited by law or custom. Yet in 1789 the country adopted a constitution in which God does not appear except as part of a date, and the first amendment to this constitution, adopted two years later, prohibits Congress from making any law respecting the establishment of religion or forbidding the free exercise thereof. No state has since been admitted to the union, not even the State of Deseret which eventually came in as Utah, that supports a church establishment.

I next note that in 1607 all writing was consciously within the Christian tradition. Even the swashbuckling Captain John

4

Smith, in his *True Relation* of 1608, recovers his health by God's assistance. In this narrative God sends Captain Newport to rescue the colony and assists Captain Smith toward a peace treaty with the Indians. The Pilgrims were devout dissenters: in his *History of Plymouth* Governor Bradford says they spent the night before sailing to America in friendly entertainment and Christian discourse, and when they arrived off Cape Cod, they drew up the famous Mayflower Compact in the name of God, declaring that "having undertaken, for the glorie of God, and advancemente of the Christian faith, and honour of our king and countrie" to settle in the New World, the subscribers did mutually "in the presence of God" set their names to the document. We read later in Bradford that the English were preserved from the smallpox, which carried off most of the Indians around them "by the marvellous goodness and providence of God," an explanation that strikes us as more devout than scientific. John Winthrop's *History of New England*—really a history of the Massachusetts Bay colony—is studded with passages about God's providence. Here are two:

Two little girls of the governor's family were sitting under a great heap of logs, plucking of birds, and the wind driving the feathers into the house, the governor's wife caused them to remove away. They were no sooner gone, but the whole heap of logs fell down in the place, and had crushed them to death, if the Lord, in his special providence, had not delivered them.

In this case providence is benign; in the second it is not:

Two men servants to one Moodye, of Roxbury, returning in a boat from the windmill, struck upon the oyster bank. They went out to gather oysters, and not making fast their boat, when the flood came, it floated away, and they were both drowned, although they might have waded out on either side, but it was an evident judgement of God upon them, for they were wicked persons.

Massachusetts Bay became a theocratic state, a common-wealth in which the civil government looked for advice and direction to the clergy. Titles of books like the *Wonder-Working Providence of Sions Savior in New England, An Essay for the Recording of Illustrious Providences, The Day of Doom,* and *Magnalia Christi Americana* (that is, the great deeds of Christ wrought in America) illustrate the interfusion of Christian belief with literature.

But though colonies like Pennsylvania and Georgia were later founded from the best of religious motives, neither life nor literature could be maintained at the high pitch of the early decades in New England. The second generation is less devout than the first, the third less devout than the second, as worldly considerations of trade, status, war, and politics become prominent. In Jamestown in 1610 Governor De La Warr could march the entire colony into church to hear two sermons on Sunday and one on Thursday, but by 1763 Devereux Jarratt, recently installed as the Anglican rector of Bath in Dinwiddie County, lamented that few of his parishioners were acquainted with Christian principles and that it was "as if the people had never seen a church or heard a sermon in their lives." Increasingly in New England during the colonial period the ministers so regularly lamented the decline of religion that the historian Perry Miller has applied the term "jeremiad" to these annual complaints. It is always difficult to estimate the truth of ecclesiastical lamentations, but as wealth increased along the Atlantic seaboard, religion became more and more a matter of morality rather than of salvation. The story is complex, but the conservatives had to make their concessions to liberalism, as in the case of Arminianism, and toleration was extended to Quakers, Baptists, Methodists, Moravians, even in time to Roman Catholics.

6

Charles Carroll of Carrollton in Maryland signed the Declaration of Independence without being called a worshipper of the Scarlet Woman of Babylon, and in Boston at the end of the eighteenth century Bishop Cheverus received an annuity from the Great and General Court for his work as a Catholic missionary among the Indians, President John Adams headed a list of subscribers to build the good bishop a church, Cheverus helped to found the Boston Athenaeum, and counted among his friends Harrison Gray Otis, Lemuel Shaw (father-in-law of Herman Melville), Josiah Quincy, and the elder Channing.

All this is a far cry from the declaration of Increase Mather in 1669 that the Catholic Church is the "Roman Anti-Christ," or that of Edward Wigglesworth in 1757 that it is filled with "Heresies, Superstitions, Cruelties, Idolatries, and other crying Wickednesses," or that of William Hobby in 1758 that it is the "Mother of Harlots," or that of Nathaniel Appleton in 1760 that it is the "*Abomination of the Earth.*"

Religious history during the one hundred and eighty-two years that stretch from Jamestown to the Federal Constitution is complex, and I cannot do justice to it. Ralph Barton Perry observes that Christianity absorbed and translated into its own terms two great articles of the pessimism which represented the last, if not the profoundest, word of the ancient wisdom: a distrust of appetite, the irreconcilable enemy of the moral will; and the conviction that wealth, power, and social station are vanity. But the natural resources of the New World whetted men's appetites; and in a rapidly evolving social pattern wherein wealth, power, and status could be achieved by all sorts of persons, these desirable things could not be dismissed as mere vanity. Calvinism was essentially aristocratic in that it divided the human race into the few who were saved and the many who were damned. It may be, as Parrington remarked, that the seeds of democracy were sown at Plymouth when that little colony granted land in fee simple and so helped create an independent yeomanry that could not be managed on aristocratic principles and saw no reason for damnation. The hold of Calvinism was weakened by the growth of secularism—that is, of commerce, war, politics, and science. Paradoxically enough, it was further weakened by an effort to buttress religion against the attrition of wealth and the celebration of ignorance. The celebration of ignorance, even among the clergy, was one of the results of that confused and contradictory movement in the second quarter of the eighteenth century known as the Great Awakening.

The Great Awakening had two origins. One was local, and is exemplified both in Virginia and in New England. The New England episode is famous. Jonathan Edwards thought he could simultaneously move the hearts of his people and bring Calvinism back to its pride of place in Northampton, but he lost the confidence of his flock and had to retire to Stockbridge, then virtually a frontier village among the Indians.

But the Great Awakening proper, by no means confined to the Calvinists, was the work of itinerant preachers like John Wesley, George Whitefield, and Gilbert Tennent, and was by and by to be carried on by exhorters and organizers like Francis Asbury, Lorenzo Dow, and eventually Billy Sunday. These men preached everywhere their exhortations directed to the emotions. A common result was crowd hysteria—shrieks, faintings, jerks, and general convulsiveness; and since no great theological lore was required, many sects—for example, the primitive Baptists—pointed out that the twelve apostles were not products of a divinity school and argued that theological learning was a hindrance to the free flow of the Spirit. All this shocked the conservatives. The last time Harvard College officially participated in a religious controversy was apparently in 1744 when that institution issued a testimony against the conduct of the Rev. George Whitefield.

An inevitable result of the Great Awakening was an increase in the tension between the standing order in any colony and the populace at large. Since immigration into America had come to include Scotch-Irish, Germans, and various other peoples; and since after 1765 (the year of the Stamp Act) dispute between the mother country and the colonies grew steadily more heated, conservative religious establishments—the standing order in Connecticut or the Anglican Church in Virginia—inevitably lost power and prestige. Anglican and Methodist clergymen fled to England. The pattern of religion in the rebellious colonies became more and more kaleidoscopic, while a new organizing element appeared in the growth of rationalism.

Rationalism had been increased by contacts between colonial leaders and officers of the British forces during the Seven Years' War. American interest in contemporary European science and European philosophy steadily developed. The conviction grew among the gentry that the earth was made for the happiness of man, and on the frontiers the same assumption prevailed. It followed that religious creeds which insisted upon human depravity seemed per se wrong-headed and that patterns of thought which insisted upon the possibility of social happiness in America and upon the potential freedom and comfort of its inhabitants gained ground.

When Tom Paine wrote in the "Appendix" to *Common Sense* that

9

the birthday of a new world is at hand, and a race of men, perhaps
as numerous as all Europe contains, are to receive their portion of
freedom from the events of a few months,

when he wrote in the third *American Crisis* paper that a continent has a natural right to independence and that

to deny such a right would be a kind of atheism against nature,

when he declared in the thirteenth *Crisis:*

To see it in our power to make a world happy—to teach mankind
the art of being so—to exhibit, on the theatre of the universe a
character hitherto unknown—and to have, as it were, a new creation intrusted to our hands, are honors that command reflection,
and can neither be too highly estimated, nor too gratefully received,

he was not merely repudiating the doctrine of human depravity
in the name of the republic, he was expressing what scores of
Americans were coming to believe about the destiny of the
United States.

III

In selecting Thomas Paine as the representative American
writer of the Revolutionary and post-Revolutionary decades I
am aware that there were greater thinkers than he. Both Franklin
and Jefferson, who tended to share his religious views, or most
of them, are more solid characters and greater men. Moreover,
Paine spent only twenty of his seventy-three years in America,
and of these twenty, the last period, from 1802 to 1810, was
negligible, for his countrymen had virtually repudiated him. In
addition to these difficulties, *The Age of Reason*, the principal
expression of his religious views, was written in France between
1793 and 1796. One has also to combat the Tom Paine legend,
exemplified in a famous phrase of Theodore Roosevelt, who

called him a filthy little atheist. Paine's personal habits were cleanly enough, he was not little, since he stood five feet nine inches high, about the same stature as Roosevelt, and as for his atheism, the first sentence in Paine's "Profession of Faith" in *The Age of Reason* reads:

I believe in one God, and no more; and I hope for happiness beyond this life.

Finally I must concede that insofar as Paine was an original thinker, his originality did not lie in his religious views, which were standard deism, but in some of his economic notions; for example, his pamphlet entitled *Agrarian Justice*, which in a mild way anticipates the ideas of Henry George.

Nevertheless he was, and is, a commanding literary figure. Born in England and receiving nothing beyond a grammar school education, he became the greatest propagandist in American literary history. His style shows what can be done with our language when it is written by what Walt Whitman would call a powerful uneducated person. His principal writings, still in print, have sold by the tens of thousands of copies, and he was, in succession to Franklin, the American author who made the greatest impression upon the European world of his time. Like Franklin, he was an inventor; like Jefferson and Franklin he was an amateur of science; and like Jefferson he had profound faith in the people. He was at one time secretary to the Committee on Foreign Affairs of the Continental Congress. An American citizen, he was charged with sedition by the British in 1792, and after making a violent speech to the Society of the Friends of Liberty, he escaped across the channel to France, where, though he could not speak French, he had been elected a member of the National Assembly from four districts. In Paris he served on a committee to write a new constitution and he tried to prevent the execution of Louis XVI. Though he was a member of the National Assembly, he was imprisoned for almost a year and was in danger of being executed. He was rescued in November, 1794, through the intervention of Monroe, then the American minister to France, but remained in France until the autumn of 1802, when, worn and weary, he returned to the United States only to face the ostracism of friends of Christianity. He died in 1809 in New Rochelle, New York. But in 1819 his bones were removed to Liverpool. What happened to the earthly remains of the great penman of the American Revolution nobody knows, though in 1849 an empty coffin bearing a silver plate inscribed "Thomas Paine, died June 8, 1809, aged 72" was known to exist, and in 1854 a Unitarian minister claimed he owned the skull and the right hand of the man who wrote:

These are the times that try men's souls.

Paine's principal writings are the great pamphlet, *Common Sense*, first published in Philadelphia, January 10, 1776; *The American Crisis*, a series of essays, thirteen numbered consecutively (with obvious reference to the thirteen original states), and three extra numbers, published in this country between 1776 and 1783; *The Rights of Man*, Paine's defense of the French Revolution against Burke's *Reflections on the French Revolution*, published by Paine in London in two parts in 1791 and 1792; and *The Age of Reason*, first printed in Paris in 1794. *The Age of Reason* is in two parts, and a third part, which exists only in fragments, was planned. Paine's minor writings, which touch on everything from the rights of women to the cause of yellow fever, show how thoroughly Paine was an eighteenth-century genius. In the Age of the Enlightenment even greater thinkers than Paine were prepared to discuss almost any question, since they believed that any problem could be reduced by rational analysis to a few simple and fundamental components.

In attempting to get at Paine's religious views we must first of all deal with his prose style, a style like that of William Cobbett, his great British contemporary, or H. L. Mencken, his influential American successor, vigorous, clear, idiosyncratic, and biased. No one has to read one of Paine's sentences twice. But he always has the air of writing in public. Queen Victoria once complained of Gladstone that he addressed her as if she were a public meeting, and Paine shares this characteristic. He addresses the populace. The common man is not likely to misunderstand him, but the elite reader may in time come to distrust this brilliancy of diction, this rhetorical manipulation. Here is Paine's weakness. But he is what the Irish call a word-spinner, and seldom in American literature has there been one more adroit. His instrument is, like Emerson's, the sentence, and on occasion he makes the individual sentence ring like a fire alarm. These are examples:

Society is produced by our wants and governments by our wickedness.

Nothing but Heaven is impregnable to vice.

The heathen paid divine honors to their deceased kings, and the Christian world improved on the plan by doing the same to their living ones.

We fight not to enslave, but to set a country free, and to make room upon the earth for honest men to live in.

Through all the vocabulary of Adam, there is no such animal as a duke or a count; neither can we connect any idea to the words.

And a final example:

Independence is my happiness, and I view things as they are, without regard to place or person; my country is the world, and my religion is to do good.

These assertions, compact and unqualified, have their immediate appeal, but we often have to look behind them to see what Paine really had in mind.

Paine's explanation of things as they are divides into two sharply contrasted paradigms of truth and error. On the one hand is the rational universe, creation of a rational deity everywhere recognizable in His creation, a universe plainly intended for the happiness of mankind on some sort of equalitarian basis in which monarchy and tradition shall have no part. In this admirably planned universe every man has natural liberty. This natural liberty can be made to pass smoothly into civil liberty in states wherein the simple voice of nature and of reason will be paramount, and if controversies arise, men will have but to think, when they can neither act wrongly nor be misled. Government, he says, is nothing more than a national association acting on the principles of society, which are given by God. The great glory of the American Revolution was that it returned to principle; the great glory of the American constitution is that it rests on universal principles of reason, an example to the British and the French and, for that matter, to all mankind. The God of Newton is also the God of Montesquieu, the God of the constitutional convention, and the God of Thomas Paine. All others are false beside him.

I have already cited the first article in Paine's expression of religious belief: he believes in one God and in happiness beyond the grave. Here is the second article:

I believe in the equality of man; and I believe that religious duties consist in doing justice, loving mercy, and endeavoring to make our fellow-creatures happy.

Clearly this sentiment has been influenced by the great passage in Micah:

14

What doth the Lord require of thee? Only to do justly, and to love mercy, and to walk humbly with thy God.

Paine's statement is so admirable, one wonders how the black legend about him arose. It is only when we turn to the other half of Paine's creed that we see why he became one of the most controversial figures in our literary history:

I do not believe in the creed professed by the Jewish Church, by the Roman Church, by the Greek Church, by the Turkish Church, by the Protestant Church, nor by any church that I know of. My own mind is my own church.

All national institutions of churches, whether Jewish, Christian, or Turkish, appear to me no other than human inventions, set up to terrify and enslave mankind, and monopolize power and profit.

I do not mean by this declaration to condemn those who believe otherwise; they have the same right to their belief that I have to mine. But it is necessary to the happiness of man that he be mentally faithful to himself. Infidelity does not consist in believing, or in disbelieving; it consists in professing to believe what he does not believe.

It is impossible to calculate the moral mischief, if I may so express it, that mental lying has produced to society.

Even this statement, if Paine had left it at that, might not have created a storm of obloquy. But Paine was incapable of defensive warfare. He wanted always to carry the war into the enemy's territory, and this he did in a manner calculated to annoy not merely the ministry but all Jewish and Christian believers. Both the churches and the Bible he made points of vehement attack. This attack has to be examined if we are to understand the legend of Paine.

Paine centers his fire upon three institutions supported by a false theology: monarchy and aristocracy, an established church, and the Bible considered as a sacred text. He blames the ancient Jews for copying the customs of the heathen, since for three thousand years after Moses, Paine says, the government of the Jews was a kind of republic except when the Almighty intervened. When the Jews proposed to make a king of Gideon, that hero refused, saying the Lord would reign over them; but when monarchy was established despite the protests of Samuel, Paine interpolates:

By which we see that bribery, corruption, and favouritism are the standing vices of kings.

Kings have laid the world in blood and ashes. The history of all monarchies he calls a

disgustful picture of human wretchedness, and the accidental respite of a few years' repose.

The first king was a thief. Bands of robbers, having parcelled out the world into dominions, quarreled with each other, for

what it first attained by violence, was considered by others lawful to be taken. . . . It was ruffian torturing ruffian.

The absurdity of hereditary monarchy soon appears: to render it consistent with government, the next monarch in succession should not be born a child but a man at once, and that man a Solomon. As for divine right, it is as bad as an established church:

the key of St. Peter, and the key of the Treasury, became quartered on one another, and the wondering, cheated multitude worshipped the invention.

And a hereditary aristocracy?

By the universal economy of nature it is known, and by the instance of the Jews it is proved, that the human species has a tendency to degenerate, in any small number of persons, when separated from the general stock of society, and intermarrying constantly with each other.

The amusing discrepancy between accepting a supernatural sanction of republican government in ancient Israel, by which Paine means the era of the judges, and denying a supernatural sanction to Solomon and David may spring from Paine's declaration that his own mind was his own church, but more likely comes from the fact that to a propagandist any stick will do to beat the dog with.

Paine's attack on established churches need not detain us long. It follows the same rhetorical pattern. Every national church or religion

has established itself by pretending some special mission from God, communicated to certain individuals;

this he contrasts with his own doctrine that the only indispensable duty of government is to protect all conscientious professors of religion. I believe, he says,

It is the will of the Almighty that there should be a diversity of religious opinions among us. It affords a larger field for our Christian kindness.

Paine reserves his fiercest language for the Bible as a sacred book, the foundation of all the errors of religion, government, and society. As Paine had no command of the tongues, the Bible was for him the King James version, and over this he brooded until its discrepancies became an obsession with him. In his earlier writings he frequently employs biblical allusions and examples to enforce a point of propaganda; in *The Age of Reason*, subtitled "An Investigation of True and Fabulous Theology," he finds most of the Bible fabulous and regrets that the work of Jewish poets was bound up in it. The Bible is filled with absurdities, obscene stories, voluptuous debaucheries, cruel and torturous executions, and unrelenting vindictiveness; it is scarcely anything but a history of the grossest vices and a collection of the most paltry and contemptible tales.

He ridicules the story of the temptation of Eve, which gives the world over to Satan, an episode which, he says, makes the transgressor triumph and the Almighty fall. He cannot credit the Mosaic account of creation. He finds it absurd that Jesus Christ, this "virtuous and . . . amiable man," supposed to be celestially begotten, is so engendered because Eve had eaten an apple. It is impossible, he declares, to conceive a story more derogatory to the Almighty, more inconsistent with His wisdom, more contradictory to His power, than this story is. Since it appears that the apostle Thomas did not believe the resurrection,

and, as they say, would not believe without having ocular and manual demonstration himself, *so neither will I,*

and Paine puts the last phrase in italics.

As to the Christian system of faith, it appears to me a species of Atheism—a sort of religious denial of God.

His denunciation rises to a kind of brassy climax in this paragraph from the "Conclusion."

The most detestable wickedness, the most horrid cruelties, and the greatest miseries that have afflicted the human race have had their origin in this thing called revelation, or revealed religion. It has been the most dishonorable belief against the character of the Divinity, the most destructive to morality and the peace and happiness of man that ever was propagated since man began to exist.

It is better, far better, that we admitted, if it were possible, a thousand devils to roam at large, and to preach publicly the doctrine of devils, if there were any such, than that we permitted one such imposter and monster as Moses, Joshua, Samuel and the Bible prophets, to come up with the pretended word of God in his mouth and have credit among us.

Small wonder that Tom Paine, in the religious reaction against the French Revolution which swept the country after 1793, was regarded by pious Americans as himself a devil preaching a devilish doctrine.

IV

What, then, did Paine believe? Eloquently he presents a theory of deism toward the conclusion of Part One of *The Age of Reason*, and it is presumably this expression of faith in a rational God, a rational universe, and rational human beings that keeps him a living force in American thought and literature.

The word of God, says Paine, is in the creation we behold. This creation speaks a universal language, independent of human speech. Do we wish to contemplate the power of God? We see it in the immensity of the creation. Do we want to contemplate His wisdom? We see it in the unchangeable order by which the incomprehensible whole is governed. Do we want to contemplate His munificence? We see it in the abundance with which He fills the earth—the doctrine of plenitude. Do we want to contemplate His mercy? We see it in His not withholding that abundance even from the unthankful. Can one by searching find out God? Yes, says Paine. I did not make myself, I know I have existence, and I search in things for a cause and find none. Can I find out the Almighty to perfection? No, answers Paine, He is incomprehensible.

But incomprehensibility in Paine's vocabulary is a word of specialized meaning, for two pages later he writes:

That which is now called natural philosophy, embracing the whole circle of science, of which astronomy occupies the chief place, is the study of the works of God, and of the power and wisdom of God in His works, and is the true theology.

Religion being for Paine a belief in God and the practice of moral truth, he thinks that religion can have no place for mystery. Mystery, for him, is a kind of pious fraud; priesthoods have, by using the word *mystery*, corrupted religion into a fog of mysteries, and miracles followed as an occasional auxiliary. The former, writes Paine in a characteristic passage, served to bewilder the mind, the latter to puzzle the senses. The one was the lingo, the other the legerdemain. To make religious belief depend upon miracles is to degrade the Almighty into the character of a showman playing tricks to amuse and make the people stare and wonder.

If we put aside Paine's cantankerousness, his tendency to score a debater's victory, and his childish obsession with the contradictions in the English Bible, which he seems to regard as something dictated to King James, we may, I think, conclude that what Paine was trying to do was to equip America with a forward-looking religion. For him deism and democracy went hand in hand. Nor is it extraordinary that he should make this attempt. A critical reading of the Declaration of Independence will show that it appeals not to a Christian deity but to the "Laws of Nature and of Nature's God." It speaks of "divine Providence" only in the last sentence, but not before it has announced that independence must come about in the "Course of human events" and laid an appeal before the "Supreme Judge of the World'" to pass upon the "rectitude" of American intentions. Since all other vestiges of European despotism were to be wiped away, why retain Christian orthodoxy with its emphasis upon human sin and human weakness, the aristocracy of the elected few and the hopeless condition of the many who were damned? Law, education, medicine were to be revolutionized in the young republic, and there was even talk about the desirability of a new language, since English was the language of King George. Why not a fresh start in religion? Why not a new form of faith? A republican religion?

Paine was not alone. The redoubtable Ethan Allen of Vermont published in 1784 a clumsy book entitled *Reason the Only Oracle of Man*, which was as unkind to the King James Bible as was Paine. The godly pointed with satisfaction to a fire that destroyed all but thirty copies of this pronouncement, which, nevertheless, had some vogue, for an abridged edition appeared in 1836 and another in 1854. In the 1790's Elihu Palmer, a member of Phi Beta Kappa from Dartmouth College, actively promoted deism through book and pamphlet, magazine and meeting; to him "Moses, Mahomet, and Jesus can lay as little claim to moral merit, or to the character of the benefactors of mankind, as any three men that ever lived upon the face of the earth." They were all of them "imposters"—a judgment which, so far as Jesus is concerned, went far beyond that of Paine. Various societies were formed, including one called the Society of Ancient Druids, which, according to A. Adolf Koch, attempted to return to the pure source of all religion, the worship of the sun. In the colleges the smart thing to do was to read Paine and Voltaire, and it should not be forgotten that Stephen Girard named his finest sailing vessels *Montesquieu*, *Rousseau*, and *Voltaire*, and when he founded Girard College in Philadelphia forbade anybody in clerical garb to set foot on the grounds or in the building.

But republican religion did not prevail. The excesses of the French Revolution horrified many supporters, who pointed to the Reign of Terror as the inevitable consequence of worshipping either a rational deity or the goddess of reason. Orthodoxy rallied and counterattacked. Men like the great Timothy Dwight of Yale satirized deism in a poem entitled *The Triumph of Infidelity*, discoursed endlessly on the genuineness of the New Testament and the moral dangers of an infidel philosophy, and Dwight, after he became president of Yale, repeated every four years a series of sermons directed at the undergraduates, discourses that were posthumously published in five volumes as *Theology Explained and Defended*. In the back country traveling evangelists called men to repentance; and the rigors of Jonathan Edwards' theology were revived and extended by the Rev. Samuel Hopkins, an abolitionist and a dull preacher, who nevertheless wrote endless theological volumes, of which the *System of Doctrines Contained in Divine Revelation, Explained and Defended*, published in two volumes in 1793, though it taught disinterested benevolence, is forever tagged with the phrase that a Christian should be glad to be damned for the greater glory of God. A genuine religious reaction seemed to dim the glory of the age of the Founding Fathers.

Such, at least, is the opinion of Herbert Schneider, the best historian of American philosophy, who writes that the American Enlightenment faded like a dream.

Its ideas were soon repudiated or corrupted, its plans for the future were buried, and there followed on its heels a thorough and passionate reaction against its ideals and assumptions. . . . Its great themes—natural rights, religious liberty, liberal religion, free thought, universal progress and enlightenment—how soon they had a hollow sound!

Both Thomas Paine and Thomas Jefferson lost repute in this period of philosophic and religious reaction.

And yet Paine and Jefferson remain persistently alive, Jefferson perhaps more so than Paine. But Paine is the principal ancestor of the radical fringe in American religious opinion.

Writers and orators like Robert C. Ingersoll, who stumped the country with an oration on "The Mistakes of Moses," agnostics like H. L. Mencken and Clarence Darrow, scholars like Philip S. Foner, keep the Paine tradition alive. The existence of organizations like the Free Religious Association of Boston and the Humanist Society of America owes something to his brashness. He is taught, though cautiously taught, in the schools and colleges. If his belief in reason fails to appeal to literary workers who have made American citizens out of Freud and Jung, his belief in science, both pure and applied, is something that modern astronomers, physicists, and engineers do not find unsympathetic. The secularization that has taken place in what were formerly church-related colleges is, in some sense, in the Paine tradition and, I suspect, our studies in comparative religion may bring a ghostly smile to his lips if, as he hoped, he is enjoying happiness beyond this life. Finally, our struggles toward racial equality and against segregation ought to remind us of the author of *The Rights of Man*, who wrote:

Man has no property in man; neither has any generation a property in the generations which are to follow,

and who said:

Under how many subtilties, or absurdities, has the divine right to govern been imposed on the credulity of mankind.

❖ II ❖

LANDSCAPE AS RELIGION: IRVING,
BRYANT, COOPER

I

WERE THESE LECTURES devoted to pursuing both the history of American religion and the development of American literature, it would be proper at this juncture to sketch the rich, if confused, story of religious life in the United States in the first half of the nineteenth century. In so doing one would have to touch upon the proliferation and growth of various evangelical sects; upon the enlargement of church membership in all religions; upon the increase in Catholics and the rising tide of anti-Catholic feeling culminating in the temporary triumph of the Know-Nothing Party in the East; upon the relation of religion to the industrial proletariat in the cities and to slaves in the South; upon the creation of new religious sects such as the Millerites, the Mormons, and the Spiritualists; upon the relation, official and unofficial, of churches to education in the United States; upon the split created in leading Protestant denominations by the slavery question; upon the Americanization of the revival movement, which produced the camp-meeting and the professionalizing of the revivalist exhorter; upon the development of the Sunday school; and upon much else.

I shall turn, however, to the treatment of landscape by certain writers in America during the first half of the nineteenth century and to the implications of these treatments for religious belief. Were there time, I should at this point dwell upon the philosophy of nature underlying the landscapes of the Hudson River School of American painters, a group with whom the so-called Knickerbocker writers had many affiliations. Possibly the most philosophic of the artists was Thomas Cole, who held not merely that landscape should be representational but also that it should express a noble ideal, which, for Cole and many of his contemporaries, meant that the painting should imply the grandeur of the Creator or give a sense of historical process or even do both. Since there were no historical ruins in America comparable to those in Italy—a favorite complaint—the painting must remind the spectator that he was in God's hands, and this commonly implied that the vastness, purity, and sublimity of the unspoiled landscape or, at most, landscape just submitting to agriculture, would by an association of ideas rouse in the viewer thoughts of the greatness and goodness of God. Cole, of course, went so far as to turn landscape into allegory, but even in painters less inclined to figurative expressiveness, craftsmanship was supposed simultaneously to represent the natural scene and indicate that landscape was the work of an almighty hand.

Formal literary description of American landscape was a relatively late development. What seems to me the first formal American landscape in literature did not appear in print until Jefferson described the confluence of the Potomac and the Shenandoah in his *Notes on Virginia*, which did not receive American publication until 1788. The three leading members of the Knickerbocker group, however—Washington Irving, William Cullen Bryant, and James Fenimore Cooper—made formal landscape passages part of their total response to American life. They differed importantly among themselves.

Here, for example, is a passage on the American landscape from Irving's *The Sketch Book*, first published in 1819–20:

I visited various parts of my own country; and had I been merely a lover of fine scenery, I should have felt little desire to seek elsewhere its gratification, for on no country have the charms of nature been more prodigally lavished. Her mighty lakes, like oceans of liquid silver; her mountains, with their bright aerial tints; her valleys, teeming with wild fertility; her tremendous cataracts, thundering in their solitudes; her boundless plains, waving with spontaneous verdure; her broad deep rivers, rolling in solemn silence to the ocean; her trackless forests, where vegetation puts forth all its magnificence; her skies, kindling with the magic of summer clouds and glorious sunshine;—no, never need an American look beyond his own country for the sublime and beautiful of natural scenery.

The most obvious quality in this rhetorically effective paragraph is that it springs from patriotism. But over and beyond the national note there are three other dominant themes: the idea of sublimity, the idea of plenitude, and the idea of dynamism. Nothing stands still, all is active, everything is in abundance, and all is vast. Sublimity, plenitude, and dynamism are certainly attributes of deity, but Irving omits something. We can best see what is omitted if we go back to a passage by Jonathan Edwards in the preceding century:

So that, when we are delighted with flowers, meadows, and gentle breezes of wind, we may consider that we see only the emanation of the sweet benevolence of Jesus Christ. When we behold the fragrant rose and lily, we see His love and purity. So the green trees and fields, and singing of birds, are the emanation of His infinite joy and benignity. The easiness and naturalness of trees and vines are shadows of His beauty and loveliness. The crystal rivers and murmuring streams are the footsteps of His favor, grace, and beauty. When we behold the light and brightness of the sun, the golden edges of an evening cloud, or the beauteous bow, we behold the adumbration of His glory and goodness; and in the blue sky, of His mildness and gentleness. There are also many things wherein we may behold His awful majesty; in the sun in his strength, in comets, in thunder, in the hovering thunder cloud, in rugged rocks, and the brows of mountains.

This, too, is rhetorically effective, yet its effectiveness is not that of either patriotism or visual experience. Conventional phrases abound—"gentle breezes," "fragrant rose and lily," "green trees and fields," "singing of birds," "crystal rivers," "murmuring springs"—these are trite, and may be applied to any and all spring or summer landscapes. What saves the paragraph is of course Edwards' passionate sincerity. His interest is not, as it were, in external nature but in the cause of external nature, which is an "emanation" of Christ, of His "infinite joy and benignity," His "favor, grace, and beauty," and so forth. Edwards' interest is in the general operation of God in and through the universe, whereas Irving's interest lies in the particular scene as the occasion of patriotic feeling.

Irving often employs landscape as a literary device. The natural setting of tales like "Rip Van Winkle" and "The Legend of Sleepy Hollow" matters tremendously in creating that willing suspension of disbelief which is the essence of poetical faith. Nor were his landscapes confined to the Hudson Valley. He wrote three books about the Great West: *A Tour on the Prairies*, *Astoria*, and *The Adventures of Captain Bonneville*. Panoramic landscapes are found in all three. He was impressed by the magnificent distances, the melancholy, and the primal quality of the West. But nowhere do you find in Irving a sense that the primitive landscape has something to do with religious belief. Content with pure narrative, he found no presence, divine or otherwise, in the light of setting suns. What was needed was to unite the sweep and specificity of Irving's panoramic vision with the deep religious conviction of Jonathan Edwards. Something like this it was the task of William Cullen Bryant to accomplish.

II

At a dinner honoring the poet's seventieth birthday in 1864 Ralph Waldo Emerson said:

When I read the verses of popular American and English poets, I often think that they appear to have gone into the art galleries and to have seen pictures of mountains, but this man to have seen mountains. . . . This artist of ours, with deeper cunning, has subsidized every solitary grove and monument-mountain in Berkshire or the Catskills, every gleaming water, the "gardens of the desert," every water-fowl and wood-bird, the evening wind, the stormy March, the song of the stars—has suborned every one of these to speak for him, so that there is no feature of day or night in the country which does not, to a contemplative mind, recall the name of Bryant.

There is something charming in this parochial identification of all the mountains in the United States with the Catskills and the Berkshires, and all the water with that in New England, but Emerson puts us on the right track for understanding the poet.

As a major writer Bryant has virtually disappeared except in the schools. This is too bad, for he gives us a significant reading of the cosmos. The decline of interest in him is due to various reasons, of which two are important: iconography, and our current dislike of literary description. The portrait of Bryant that is forever being reproduced is that of Bryant as an old man—a venerable sage something like one of the Hebrew prophets as imagined by Michelangelo. It is hard to think of this face as ever having been that of a fiery youth, full of passion and conflict, writing as his first important poem a satire on Mr. Jefferson's Embargo Act. As for literary descriptions, they are no longer fashionable in our introspective and colloquial literature; and now that we have ravaged the continent, despoiled the forests, polluted the rivers, and poisoned the air, we do not want to be reminded by immortal verse of what we have had and what we have lost. Bryant perpetually reminds us of what the landscape once was and what it might still be.

This poet, so plain, so dignified, so simple, is a budget of paradoxes. His family was too poor to send him to Yale; yet when he died his estate was worth about a million dollars. He was a New England boy and youth; he became a cosmopolitan traveler in both the Old World and the New. He wrote principally of nature; but he spent most of his adult life at the desk of a newspaper editor. He favored the abolitionists, and he opposed the Darwinians. He was an infallible speller, yet he said he could never master the catechism. Perhaps for this reason this most Protestant of poets once told his wife that he thought a good Catholic quite as good as a good Calvinist. He was brought up in a Presbyterian community; but he was not baptized until he was sixty-four. He was a Unitarian who believed in the divinity of Christ. Few people, his daughter wrote, knew how religious he was; yet when he made his will he made no mention of God. He thought the course of things was in general right, but he told R. H. Dana in 1848 that he did not think any political change would create a paradise on earth and that, even if in the course of time republican institutions prevailed, unless we could find some way of inculcating obedience to the civil magistrate, republican government might vanish in the twentieth century. What is one to make of this singular mixture?

I think a clue appears in an observation made in a memorial

address delivered by Dr. Samuel Osgood before the Goethe Society in New York. The speaker remarked:

> It was said of Marcus Aurelius that he brought stoicism so near to Christianity that after him it died out and Christianity took its place. In Bryant this change was made before his death, and his poems are the record that in his life he passed from the stoic into the Christian.

This is true enough in its way; the question is how much of Bryant's view is stoic and how much of it is Christian.

Bryant composed a number of hymns, many of his other poems contain evidence of Christian values, he believed in the immortality of the soul, and, as I have indicated, though a Unitarian, he accepted the divinity of Christ. On the other hand his famous "Thanatopsis" has not the slightest trace of a Christian system, and his best lyric, "To a Waterfowl," refers only to an undefined Power that guides the bird and will, the poet hopes, guide him. This is but vaguely a Christian concept, if, indeed, it be Christian at all. It would appear that Bryant was religious by temperament—on this we have a great deal of testimony—but that his poetry is only intermittently Christian.

He has been called the poet of nature and he has been called the poet of death. Death occupies an uncommonly large space in the 13,000 lines that he wrote, but the phrase "a poet of nature" requires considerable defining. His verse is filled with specific mentions or descriptions of plants, trees, animals, bodies of water, mountains, winds, and skies—one scholar has found that Bryant mentions forty varieties of trees and over thirty kinds of flowers. These specific objects in nature occasion some of his better verse: for examples, "To the Fringed Gentian" and his charming poem on the bob-o'-link. But neither the enumeration of natural objects nor literature descriptive of them illuminates a poet's philosophy unless some deeper meaning is hinted at or stated. For example, we cannot pass beyond the enumeration of objects in one of Irving's landscapes unless or until a larger context is implied. Bryant supplies this religious context.

It seems to me that Bryant is a poet of process—of an eternal movement, sometimes thought of as cyclical, sometimes as spiral, which he finds in the universe and which he usually thinks of as divinely directed, though the director is only sparsely a Christian God. In many important pieces by Bryant the poem goes no farther than stating or implying that the universe means largely and means well. Christianity becomes more often a symbol of process than the cause of it; and for that reason, though the man Bryant may have passed from the stoic into the Christian, the poetry follows no such uniform development.

Stoicism, like Christianity, is a word of many meanings and as a philosophy alters from age to age. I think, however, it is generally true of the stoic point of view, first that knowledge of the cosmos is realized by virtuous action; second, that all existence is probably within the knowable universe; third, that God, or the gods, or the world soul is to the universe what the soul is to man; fourth, that justice is a general, not a local concept; and fifth, that the stoic has a deep conviction of the weakness and misery of man, of the ineluctability of evil, and of the vanity of life, but that he tries to attain resignation to the course of things because the course of things is somehow supremely directed, probably by divinity. Such, at any rate, is what I make of the hymn of Cleanthes, which addresses Zeus as the sovereign of nature and says, among other things:

Thee all this universe, as it rolls circling round the earth, obeys wheresoever thou dost guide. . . . No work upon earth is wrought apart from thee . . . nor through the divine ethereal sphere, nor upon the sea; save only those deeds that wicked men do in their own folly. . . . Thou hast so fitted all things together, the good with the evil, so that there might be one eternal law governing all.

And I read in the *Meditations* of Marcus Aurelius:

Death is such as generation is, a mystery of nature, a composition of the same elements, and a decomposition into the same; and altogether not a thing of which any man should be ashamed, for it is not contrary to . . . the reason of our constitution.

And a little later is this famous passage:

Everything harmonizes with me which is harmonious to thee, O Universe. Nothing for me is too early nor too late, which is in due time for thee. Everything is fruit to me, which thy seasons bring, O Nature: from thee are all things, in thee are all things, to thee all things return. The poet says, Dear city of Cecrops and wilt not thou say, Dear city of Zeus?[1]

It seems to me that Bryant combines, from his reading of classical antiquity, the melancholy and the grandeur of the Virgilian sense for history and the stoic's belief that there is an intelligible purpose in the universe, even if man cannot wholly comprehend that purpose. All this he tried to fuse with Christianity, but I think it true that Bryant was not so much the poet of nature or of death or of Christian principles as he was a premature existentialist. These ideas are not incompatible. Bryant's constant cry is that man is alone in a cosmos too vast for his comprehending except as process, some imperfect glimpse of which he may attain.

Here, for example, is a poem called "Earth," published in 1836 when the poet was forty years old:

A midnight black with clouds is in the sky;
I seem to feel, upon my limbs, the weight

[1] For this passage on stoicism, except for Marcus Aurelius, I have followed the sensible article on the stoics by R. D. Hicks in the *Encyclopaedia Britannica*, 14th ed.

Of its vast brooding shadow. All in vain
Turns the tired eye in search of form; no star
Pierces the pitchy veil; no ruddy blaze,
From dwellings lighted by the cheerful hearth,
Tinges the flowering summits of the grass.
No sound of life is heard, no village hum,
Nor measured tramp of footstep in the path,
Nor rush of wind, while, on the breast of Earth,
I lie and listen to her mighty voice:
A voice of many tones—sent up from streams
That wander through the gloom, from woods unseen
Swayed by the sweeping of the tides of air,
From rocky chasms where darkness dwells all day,
And hollows of the great invisible hills,
And sands that edge the ocean, stretching far
Into the night—a melancholy sound!
O Earth! dost thou too sorrow for the past
Like man thy offspring?

This poem was written in Italy. It reviews the wickedness of
history, the wreckage of nations, and the littleness of man, and
concludes by asking what shall cleanse the bosom of the earth of
all these horrors. The answer ought to be the Providence of God
if the Christian belief is correct, but this is not the answer of the
poem. There we read that America has a chance to write a newer
page in the great record of the world, but the last lines in the
poem are this dark ambiguity:

Shall it be fairer? Fear and friendly Hope,
And Envy, watch the issue, while the lines,
By which thou shalt be judged, are written down.

This clearly is nothing like Tom Paine's triumphant shout
that as kings go down, republics will rise, nor does it in the least
resemble Tennyson's hope in *In Memoriam* about a Christian
cry across the conquered years. Instead, it is, like "Thanatopsis,"
a statement of process, an attempt at resignation. Other poems

by this writer—for example, "The Ages," read at a Phi Beta Kappa meeting—are less melancholy, but though in "The Ages" a new civilization is to spring up in the United States, Bryant cannot forget that the Indians are doomed through no fault of their own and that Europe is still a prey to what he calls "sterner fates." This is scarcely Christian optimism.

If we look at a poem like "Inscription for the Entrance to a Wood," we discover that the sick heart of man can be partially healed by the calm of nature. If we read Bryant's "Hymn to Death," the lesson is that in the equality of dying, justice is done, and in this knowledge virtue lies. If we read "A Forest Hymn," we find that the groves were God's first temples and that God has left as witness to His qualities the grandeur, strength, and grace of the mighty woods, a lesson parallel, I think, to the hymn of Cleanthes and the philosophy of Marcus Aurelius.

> My heart is awed within me when I think
> Of the great miracle that still goes on,
> In silence, round me—the perpetual work
> Of thy creation, finished, yet renewed
> Forever. Written on thy works I read
> The lesson of thy own eternity.
> Lo! all grow old and die—but see again
> How on the faltering footsteps of decay
> Youth presses.

There is here nothing that Zeno could have disapproved. If God scares the world with tempests and whirlwinds, the great cycle of the cosmos is not essentially disturbed.

> Life mocks the idle hate
> Of his arch-enemy Death—yea, seats himself
> Upon the tyrant's throne—the sepulchre,
> And of the triumphs of his ghastly foe
> Makes his own nourishment. For he came forth
> From thine own bosom, and shall have no end.

I repeat as relevant the sentences I quoted from Marcus Aurelius:

Everything harmonizes with me, which is harmonious with thee, O Universe. Nothing for me is too early nor too late, which is in due time for thee. Everything is fruit to me, which thy seasons bring, O Nature; from thee are all things, in thee are all things, to thee all things return.

"Thanatopsis" early proclaims what many of Bryant's later poems solemnly intone: that the wise man will reconcile himself to the vast cycle of nature. Here are some typical statements:

> . . . the cycle of eternal change,
> Which is the life of Nature, shall restore,
> With sounds and scents from all thy mighty range,
> Thee to thy birthplace of the deep once more.

The reference here is to the evening wind, in a poem of that name. In another entitled "Among the Trees" we learn that the seasons lead a life apart from the emotions of man, that the trees have in a sense no memory and no history, but that

> an unremembered Past
> Broods, like a presence, mid the long gray boughs
> Of this old tree, which has outlived so long
> The flitting generations of mankind.

The poet feels that in some vague future things may improve:

> An age when, in the eternal strife between
> Evil and Good, the Power of Good shall win
> A grander mastery; when kings no more
> Shall summon millions from the plough to learn
> The trade of slaughter, and of populous realms
> Make camps of war,

and he again has some hope for the United States, but this is neither republican enthusiasm nor fervent Christian faith. One of Bryant's most characteristic productions is "The Flood of Years," which begins:

> A mighty Hand, from an exhaustless Urn,
> Pours forth the never-ending Flood of Years
> Among the nations,

goes on to picture the nations as overwhelmed by the flood of time, regards the past as a silent ocean, a waste of waters, talks about old cities, deserted streets, and the ruin of former cultures, and hints that the "brood of Hope" may bring about eventual improvement for mankind. The poem is commonplace as philosophy, but moving as emotion. The emotional impact of the poem is what I may call one of stoic meliorism, scarcely that of triumphant Christianity.

I am somehow reminded of a poem of Rilke, "O sage, Dichter, was du tust," which is thus translated by H. F. Peters:

> Oh, tell us, poet, what you do?
> —I praise.
> But those dark, deadly devastating ways,
> how do you bear them, suffer them?
> —I praise.
> And then, the Nameless, beyond guess or gaze,
> how can you call it, conjure it?
> —I praise.
> And whence your right, in every kind of maze,
> in every mask, to remain true?
> —I praise.[2]

Nature, wrote Bryant in "The Ages," in her calm, majestic march, never falters, the world shows "the truth in her fair page," and even though in this melancholy vision ancient nations have left no memory, but only a record in the desert of

---

[2] *Rainer Maria Rilke: Masks and the Man* (Seattle, 1960), p. 34.

> columns strown
> On the waste sands, and statues fallen and cleft,
> Heaped like a host in battles overthrown;
> Vast ruins, where the mountain's ribs of stone
> Were hewn into a city; streets that spread
> In the dark earth, where never breath has blown
> Of heaven's sweet air.

Like Rilke, Bryant can exclaim: "I praise!"

In "Thanatopsis" the poet hears a still voice saying that he, too, will die, losing each "human trace." Let him reflect, however, that he will not retire alone to his eternal resting place; the magnificent couch of nature is one on which kings and patriarchs eternally repose. And how majestic is earth, even considered as a tomb!

> The hills
> Rock-ribbed and ancient as the sun,—the vales
> Stretching in pensive quietness between;
> The venerable woods—rivers that move
> In majesty, and the complaining brooks
> That make the meadows green; and, poured round all,
> Old Ocean's gray and melancholy waste.

These are the great ornaments of the tomb of man. The dead are everywhere; therefore

> when thy summons comes to join
> The innumerable caravan,

you shall not go down like a quarry slave, scourged to his dungeon, but

> sustained and soothed
> By an unfaltering trust,

lie down to pleasant dreams. Here is no trace of Christian glory.

"The Prairies" pictures a vast and tenantless landscape, yet the dead are there, and most of the poem imaginatively pictures races that passed away long before the Parthenon was built. The forms of being change; it makes no difference to the cosmos that a particular form disappears, and if the poet now hears "the sound of that advancing multitude" which is to populate the prairies and create the Middle West, this is but one phase of an eternal process.

Bryant is the poet of elemental forces—death and life, the seasons, storm and calm, the sea, the wind, the snow, but he is not a Christian "nature poet" as Whittier or Longfellow is. Indeed, if one is to save this melancholy spirit for Christian poetry, one is almost tempted to define him as a Christian who fell into the heresy of Manichaeism—that the struggle between darkness and light, between tragedy and calm, between good and evil, is his central reading of the Christian faith. It is unorthodox to say so, but I feel, in studying Bryant, that his Christianity was a piece of personal sincerity that cannot be questioned, and that so far as his world view is concerned, Christianity is for him an outward and modern symbol of an ancient and more primitive faith. And though I cannot go all the way with Albert McLean in his admirable study of Bryant, I think this paragraph by him helps us to place the poet in his temporal and intellectual context:

The failure of our contemporary readers to respond to Bryant's pious Nature poetry is symptomatic. Science, having long since abandoned the obvious evidences of order—such as would strike the eye of Sunday strollers or bird watchers—has left us indifferent before natural objects, save for those which overwhelm us with sensory stimuli. For the nineteenth century, however, still laboriously sifting genera and species, still pondering the enormous scale of geological ages, still deciphering the mysterious laws which govern comets, natural facts were neither too remote to be interesting nor too complex to forestall rational consideration. Thus it was that the magnificent "Creator" or "First Cause" of Newton could be glimpsed in moments of intensity, only a few paces beyond normal vision, lurking behind woodland oaks and impelling birds in their flight. . . . [In Bryant's case] not systematic thought brought him closer to God, and God closer to Nature, but mood, revery, and observation. This piety which we cannot share had its source not in logic but in experience, and only thus can it be comprehended.[3]

This is admirably said. Whether one thinks with Mr. McLean that Bryant's questing ends in piety (in the Christian sense), or with me that it goes back to a more primitive and persistent philosophy of stoicism, one thing is clear: Bryant's verse demands a more searching analysis than it has received. We have passed beyond the bias of the nineteenth century in reading him, but we have not as yet plucked out the heart of his mystery.

III

James Fenimore Cooper, to whom I turn in conclusion, is remarkable in many ways but among major American novelists he is unique in his total acceptance of trinitarian Christianity and his insistent interpretation of man and the universe in the light of this belief. The most striking example of this interest is a late novel, *The Sea Lions*, a stirring tale of adventure in the Antarctic published in 1849. Two schooners, rivals, each called *The Sea Lion*, depart from Long Island on a sealing expedition. After various encounters with storms and other incidents, they are frozen in the Antarctic ice for the winter. The captain of one vessel, by name Daggett, once the contest for pelts begins, is overcome with cupidity; through his recklessness he loses most of his crew, his vessel, and his life. During the Antarctic winter he is befriended by Captain Roswell Gardiner, who is in love with Mary Pratt, daughter of the vessel's owner. Mary is also in love with him but has refused him because, being a Unitarian,

[3] Albert F. McLean, Jr., *William Cullen Bryant* (New York, 1964), p. 58.

niece!

he does not accept the divinity of Christ. Partly under the tuition of a devout seaman named Stimson, partly out of his love for Mary, but mostly, we are asked to believe, under the influence of the vast and solemn panorama of the stars, Gardiner comes to believe in the mystery of the Christian faith. He returns, clasps Mary in his arms, and whispers

the blessed words that announced his own humble submission to the faith which accepted Christ as the Son of God.

The Sea Lions is better than this bald summary, but Cooper is explicit about what he is doing. In the preface he says:

A million . . . eyes shall pass over the firmament, on a cloudless night, and not a hundred minds shall be filled with a proper sense of the power of the dread Being that created all that is there.

Something we cannot comprehend, he thinks, lies at the root of every distinct division of natural phenomena. He insists with Pascal that the "pride of reason" is "one of the most insinuating of our foibles," and he writes the book to show how the pride of reason can be chastened in an active man.

Toward the climax of the tale Roswell Gardiner is alone, contemplating the Antarctic night.

The moon was young, but the stars gave forth a brightness that is rarely seen, except in the clear cold nights of a high latitude. Each and all of these sublime emblems of the power of God were twinkling like bright torches glowing in space; and the mind had only to endow each with its probable or known dimensions, its conjectural and reasonable uses, to form a picture of the truest sublimity, in which man is made to occupy his real position. In this world, where in a certain sense he is master, where all things are apparently under his influence . . . one gets a mistaken and frequently a fatal notion of his true place in the scale of beings who are intended to throng around the footstool of the Almighty. . . . never before had he [Roswell] been made so conscious of his own insignificance as he became while looking on the firmament that night, glowing with its bright worlds and suns, doubtless the centres of other systems in which distance swallowed up the lesser orbs.

Roswell had seen chemical experiments that produced wonderful illuminations; but faint, indeed, were the most glowing of those artificial torches, to the floods of light that came streaming out of the void, on missions of millions and millions of miles. . . . what was he himself that he should presume to set up his miserable pride of reason in opposition to a revelation supported by miracles that must be admitted to come through men inspired by the Deity or rejected altogether?

In this frame of mind Roswell was made to see that Christianity admitted no half-way belief. . . . why should not Christ be the Son of God?

. . . the necessity for the great expiation occurred to his mind. . . . Had not science gradually discovered the chemical processes by which gases could be concentrated and disengaged, the formation of one of those glittering orbs above his head would have been quite as unintelligible a mystery to him as the incarnation of the Saviour.

Although the logic by which the Antarctic night is thus made a proof of the divinity of Christ is a little to seek, the way of a novelist is not that of a metaphysician.

The sincerity of Cooper's belief that trinitarian Christianity, preferably of the Anglican or Episcopalian variety, is necessary to a good society is evident in his utopian novel, The Crater, published two years earlier. In this book Mark Woolston colonizes a volcanic island. The community gets along very well under his paternal government, himself as governor and a small elected council being the form of administration. There is only one church on the island, and that is Episcopalian. But immigrants come in, insist upon political democracy, insist upon the freedom of the press, and insist on introducing other religious sects in the name of liberty. The result is the wrecking of the utopia; and part of the damage is that after religious toleration is declared, men no longer pray to God, they pray at each other. The novel is in part a satire on communal enterprises of the Fourier or Brook Farm variety, in part a satire on American politics in the 1840's.

Cooper's Christianity has unexpected blindnesses and unexpected tolerations. He had little use for New England or for dissenters, and he equated the two. Though *The Wept of Wishton-Wish* (1829), a historical tale of seventeenth-century Connecticut, is fair enough toward the Puritans, Cooper turns David Gamut, the New England singing master in *The Last of the Mohicans*, into comic relief, and in the anti-rent novels, *Satanstoe, The Chainbearer,* and *The Redskins,* makes Jason Newcome, a New Englander transplanted to New York, a mean-minded villain. Cooper was less than enthusiastic about Catholicism; on the other hand his European novels show no great amount of hostility to that church. Finally is to be noted a certain inconsistency between Cooper's Christianity and his belief in a Hamiltonian form of the state, one resting upon government by the enlightened few. Cooper thought the cultivated and responsible English gentleman the highest type of Christian and urged that American gentlemen might pattern themselves upon him, merely liberalizing their views and avoiding the errors of a hereditary aristocracy. On the other hand, in *The Chainbearer* Cooper defines a gentleman without much reference to Christianity; for example,

he is truthful out of self-respect, and not in obedience to the will of God,

and the aged Indian chief, Susquesus, is characterized as a kind of nature's nobleman, a Christian in spirit but not in fact. And of course the characterization of Leatherstocking raises a puzzling problem of consistency.

Leatherstocking was brought up by the Moravians and constantly laments that he has had to drift away from their peaceful teaching; yet he is obviously one of nature's noblemen, described in *The Prairie* through the mouth of young Middleton in these terms:

The man I speak of was of great simplicity of mind, but of sterling worth. Unlike most of those who lived a border life, he united the better instead of the worst qualities of the two people [Indians and whites]. He was a man endowed with the choicest and perhaps rarest gift of nature; that of distinguishing good from evil. His virtues were those of simplicity, because such were the fruits of his habits, as were indeed his very prejudices. In courage he was the equal of his red associates, in warlike skill, being better instructed, their superior.

The death of Leatherstocking, narrated in the closing pages of *The Prairie*, one of the most moving scenes in all of Cooper's fiction, is curiously un-Christian; when Middleton offers to see to it that the dying trapper has a Christian headstone, the old man at first refuses, and then says:

Put no boastful words on the same, but just the name, the age, and the time of death, with something from the Holy Book, no more, no more.

Christianity here becomes identified, so to speak, with natural religion.

In truth, though the current of trinitarian Christianity, now hidden, now coming to the surface in particular novels, runs through most of Cooper's fiction, there is a parallel current equally important—a belief in natural theism. This is evident in the books by Cooper that everybody knows best—the Leatherstocking tales. Everyone remembers the impressions left on his imagination by the landscapes of these novels—the endless forests, the boundless prairies, the waters, the skies, storm and sunshine, the fertility of unspoiled nature. In these vast and primal landscapes live three kinds of human beings: Indians, Leatherstocking, and a variety of other types of the white race, most of whom are corrupted by the culture of sophisticated society. Nature in all these novels save *The Pioneers* is the unspoiled nature of Bryant.

Leatherstocking prefers the book of nature to any printed word. When in *The Last of the Mohicans* David Gamut proposes the Calvinist doctrine of election and damnation, Leatherstocking scornfully replies:

Books! . . . what have such as I, who am a warrior of the wilderness, though a man without a cross, to do with books! I never read but in one, and the words that are written there are too simple and too plain to need such schooling. . . . 'Tis open before your eyes . . . and he who owns it, is not niggard of its use. I have heard it said, that there are men who read in books, to convince themselves there is a God! I know not but man may so deform his works in the settlements, as to leave that which is clear in the wilderness, a matter of doubt among traders and priests. If any such there be, and he will follow me from sun to sun, through the windings of the forest, he shall see enough to teach him that he is a fool, and that the greatest of his folly lies in striving to rise to the level of one he can never equal, be it in goodness, or be it in power.

The paradox is that if in *The Sea Lions* Roswell Gardiner is brought by the contemplation of nature in the Antarctic to accept the mystery of Christianity, in the Leatherstocking tales the hero, though educated in Christianity, sloughs off Christian theology and subsumes the God of Christianity under the God of nature.

Nor is this all. Not once but many times Leatherstocking insists that mankind has a variety of gifts. This phrase implies more than a recognition of differences among national, racial, and tribal beliefs. Indians and white men may be individually good or bad, but each race is justified in operating within its own ethical and religious tradition. Without realizing his inconsistency Cooper comes very close to arguing like Walter Savage Landor that we are what sun and wind and water make us. In *The Pathfinder*, for example, the virtually natural religion of Natty Bumppo is superior to the Christianity of the towns, but on the other hand the natural religion of Chingachgook and the Hurons has its own ethics, often admirable, yet lacks the quality of forgiveness.

In so-called civilized life social virtue ought to rest upon the concept of Christian brotherhood—and in *Notions of an American* (1828) Cooper unexpectedly goes out of his way to pay a tribute to New England in this regard; but in the America of his prime, the competitive principle has led men during and after the Jacksonian revolution to abuse the gifts of God and ignore the fraternal principle. In the wilderness, brotherhood is a purer concept, one overriding the boundaries of any religious sect. Says the aged Leatherstocking in *The Prairie*:

Red-skin or White-skin, it is much the same. Friendship and use can tie men together in the woods as in the towns, ay, and for that matter stronger. . . . I have been a solitary man much of my time, if he can be called solitary who has lived for seventy years in the very bosom of natur', and where he could at any instant open his heart to God, without having to strip it of the cares and wickednesses of the settlements . . . and yet I have always found that intercourse with my kind was pleasant, was painful to break off, provided that the companion was brave and honest.

These admirable virtues in the natural man are, of course, not found in all Indians[4] or all woodmen, but neither Cooper nor Leatherstocking speculates importantly upon the origin of wickedness in the cosmic scheme. Yet in the wilderness man is, if he

[4] Contrary to popular belief there are very few "noble Indians" in the totality of Cooper's fiction.

be at all good, superior to municipal man. Says Leatherstocking in an earlier passage in the same novel:

Many is the hour that I've passed lying in the shades of the woods, or stretch'd upon the hills of these open fields, looking up into the blue skies, where I could fancy the Great One had taken his stand, and was solemnizing on the waywardness of man and brute below, as I myself had often look'd at the ants tumbling over each other in their eagerness, though in a way and a fashion more suited to His mightiness and power.

The resemblance of Leatherstocking's assumption to a similar one by Bryant is clear.

And like Bryant, Leatherstocking (or Cooper for him) is a believer in process. Contrast these two passages from *The Prairie*, both put in the mouth of Leatherstocking:

No, no, the garden of the Lord was the forest then, and is a forest now, where the fruits do grow and the birds do sing, according to his own wise ordering.

And then:

Time was made by the Lord, and they [civilizations] were made by man. This very spot of weeds and grass, on which you now sit, may once have been the garden of some mighty king. It is the fate of all things to ripen, and then to decay. The tree blossoms, and bears its fruit, which falls, rots, withers, and even the seed is lost!

The processes of life are, then, cyclical and the aged trapper contends that the coming of metropolitan culture is evidence that mankind is now on the downward slope. "How much," he exclaims,

has the beauty of the wilderness been deformed in two short lives! My own eyes were first opened on the shores of the Eastern sea, and well do I remember that I tried the virtues of the first rifle I ever bore, after such a march, from the door of my father to the forest, as a stripling could make between sun and sun; and that without offence to the rights or prejudices of any man who set himself up to be the owner of the beasts of the fields. Natur' then lay in its glory along the whole coast, giving a narrow strip, between the woods and the ocean, to the greediness of the settlers. And where am I now? Had I the wings of an eagle, they would tire before a tenth of the distance, which separates me from the sea, could be passed; and towns and villages, farms and highways, churches and schools, in short, all the inventions and deviltries of man, are spread across the region.

This passage could have appeared today, so far as the mention of the virtues of the wilderness are concerned, in any bulletin of the Sierra Club.

I fear that Cooper comes out on the side of religious pessimism, whether he is characterizing life in commercial capitals, or the melancholy disappearance of the Indian, the trapper, and the wilderness. In the environment of wild landscape man may achieve a simple and noble relationship to God. But in the cycle of time this naturalness gives way to the corruption of the marketplace, and few there are with enough insight into the meaning of Christianity to withstand such corruption. The cyclical quality of history is, apparently, part of the mysterious action of God, and from the point of a devout Episcopalian, which Cooper was, the ultimate comment on it is the sad wisdom of Ecclesiastes:

One generation passeth away, and another generation cometh. . . . The sun also ariseth, and the sun goeth down, and hasteth to his place where he ariseth. . . . All the rivers run into the sea, yet the sea is not full; Unto the place whither the rivers go, Thither they go again.

Few of us realize the long tradition of melancholy in American literature.

·→ III ·←·

TRANSCENDENTALISM AND EMERSON

I

THE STUDENT of American transcendentalism comes by and by to feel like Peer Gynt when that rapscallion encounters the Great Boyg. In Ibsen's poem, Peer has managed to escape from the hall of the Mountain King, but he is no sooner out of the building than he runs into the Boyg, a vast foggy creature he can neither cut through nor go around. The Boyg says to Peer:

> It's the Boyg that's unwounded, and the Boyg that was hurt.
> It's the Boyg that is dead, and the Boyg that's alive.

After struggling against this monster for a time Peer exclaims:

> Forward or back, and it's just as far;—
> Out or in, and it's just as strait!

Suddenly the Boyg rolls up and disappears. Except that it won't disappear, transcendentalism has all the foggy characteristics of the Great Boyg.

If one tries to analyze transcendentalism as a form of religious faith, one discovers that though it infiltrated some pulpits, it founded no church, formulated no creed, and produced no ministers of its own. Some believers like the eccentric Orestes A. Brownson took final refuge in Roman Catholicism, others like

Ellery Channing mistook the religion of nature for the worship of whim, and still a third group, of whom Thoreau is representative, came to disdain all formalized church services. If one approaches transcendentalism as a problem in epistemology, one is told that it originated in Kantian metaphysics, and this is true; yet Theodore Parker was almost the only transcendentalist to master German sufficiently well to read Kant in the original, and most of the others got their German philosophy at second hand from French writers like Cousin and British writers like Coleridge. Of Cousin's philosophy, however, Emerson later said there was an optical illusion in it; and when Emerson visited Coleridge in 1833, the poet-philosopher spent a good deal of time denouncing Unitarianism, the faith out of which transcendentalism arose. If one approaches the movement on the aesthetic plane, one can read a great many transcendental effusions about Art with a capital A and Soul with a capital S, but the modern reader shortly comes to feel he is paying a visit to Cloud-cuckooland. Moreover, the group included almost no painters or musicians, and, three or four great literary names aside, most of the writing done by transcendentalists is either fragmentary or inchoate. As a political force transcendentalism lent moral energy to the abolitionist cause and disturbed the complacency of the Whig mercantile interests, but it never took shape as a party, nor even as a splinter group. Transcendentalism looms large in American cultural history; its followers were nevertheless mainly confined to a small group in eastern Massachusetts and smaller groups in Ohio. Perry Miller is sympathetic to transcendentalism; yet in the preface to his anthology concerning the movement he remarks on its self-destructive tendency.

Margaret Fuller fled to Europe, violence and death; Cranch took refuge in Florence and dilettantism; Parker killed himself with overwork; Thoreau expended himself; Emerson dissolved into aphasia; Ripley subsided into disillusion; Hedge became a Harvard professor; Jones Very kept himself out of the lunatic asylum by writing verses; Brownson became a Catholic; so did Sophia Ripley; Elizabeth Peabody became a "character"; Bancroft became a politician; the Sturgis girls married; J. S. Dwight became a music critic; Ellery Channing spent a life of futility; Bronson Alcott alone endured to the end.[1]

This is amusing and partly true, and for a moment the Great Boyg seems to disappear. Even the Concord School of Philosophy, which was held in Bronson Alcott's back yard, had something amateurish and evanescent about it.

But the Boyg will not go away. A movement that nourished Emerson and in some degree Thoreau and touched the genius of Hawthorne, Melville, and James Russell Lowell cannot be ignored. All the books on American development give it space, perhaps because transcendentalism is a major phase of something even vaster—romanticism in the United States, a force the definition of which nobody can give and the boundaries of which nobody can determine.

It is probably true, as one critic has said, that transcendentalism is best understood as something indigenous to the soil from which it sprang, but no other cultural movement in our history drew on a more varied and cosmopolitan library. Transcendental reading ranged from Oriental philosophies through Plato and Jesus to Goethe, Swedenborg, Lamarck, and a Boston wholesale druggist named Sampson Reed. If George Santayana denied that Emerson was a philosopher, transcendental thought was one of the forces that undermined the Scottish Common Sense philosophy in the colleges and laissez-faire economic theory in

[1] Perry Miller, ed., The Transcendentalists: An Anthology (Cambridge, Mass., 1950), p. 14.

industry and on the stock exchange. To the pious, Emerson's "Divinity School Address" was the latest form of infidelity; but his philosophical idealism liberalized theology, freed many a soul from the terrors of Calvinism and the aridity of Unitarian orthodoxy, and helped create a Protestant ecumenical movement after the Civil War that produced such useful things as the National Council of Churches of Christ and the American Humanist Society. The aesthetics of the movement were indeed vague; yet its vitality fed the artistic and moral idealism which governed art in the United States after 1860. Alcott's Boston school experiment failed; his doctrine of the inviolability of the personality and of education as a process of unfolding latent perceptions preceded and nourished the progressive doctrine in twentieth-century education.

What is one to do amid this rich confusion? How order, how simplify, how understand? Our main interest is in Emerson; and I think the best approach will be to sketch some of the forces that brought New England transcendentalism into being, and in the light of this brief history, observe the development of Emerson's thought.

II

Transcendentalism aimed at the destruction of Calvinist theory about the depravity of human nature. But Calvinism had many phases; and transcendentalism drew upon certain important elements in Calvinist theory to feed itself. For all its rigidity Calvinism in a sense asserts the right of private judgment and individualized experience: you have to make up your own mind on probable evidence whether you are damned or elected, and to decide this grave question you have to know whether the grace of God is working within you. It was therefore possible to be both a Calvinist and a mystic; and Jonathan Edwards' *Treatise Concerning the Religious Affections*, which Emerson knew, and his *Images or Shadows of Divine Things*, which he could not know, anticipate in the one case Emerson's doctrine of ecstasy or spiritual intuition; in the other, his doctrine of the correspondence in nature between divinity and the soul.

Prosperity and equalitarianism were the enemies of this kind of Augustinian theology, and in an effort to placate these secular rivals Calvinism made a series of compromises that were in fact successive defeats. Indeed, the Bible Commonwealth was doomed from its foundation. By the time of the American Revolution, Calvinism, or some branches of it, had so weakened its traditional tenets that Christian theology tended to converge with natural religion. When in 1786 the proprietors of King's Chapel in Boston voted to drop all reference to the Trinity from the Book of Common Prayer, they created the first Unitarian church in America and freed mercantile respectability from both the fear of hell-fire and the unseemly doctrine of inherited depravity. The relation among God, man, and the universe in Unitarian circles was for a time a relation as plain and rational as the psychology of John Locke. But the difficulty in a plain and rational religion is of course that it remains plain and rational. It lacks the somber tragedy of Calvin and the mystical rapture of Edwards. In the phrase of Harvey Townsend heaven and earth had now been sundered, and the great question in men's minds was how they could be brought together again.

It was plain that they must be reunited. Rationalism, as in the cases of Hume and Holbach, had run into skepticism and thence into materialism and atheism; and the excesses of the French Revolution, which lost nothing in the reporting, were proof that godlessness might also end in a blood bath. The

worship of the Goddess of Reason was, so to speak, a parody of
The Age of Reason by Tom Paine; the fruits of deism were the
godless Reign of Terror and the satanic Napoleonic Wars. Two
years after King's Chapel went Unitarian, Timothy Dwight, the
future president of Yale, ironically dedicated his poem, *The
Triumph of Infidelity*, to Voltaire, the great image of infidelity
in the period. Here are four representative lines:

> There stood the infidel of modern breed,
> Blest vegetation of infernal seed,
> Alike no Deist, and no Christian he;
> But from all principle, all virtue free.

A little later the Anglo-Irish poet, Thomas Moore, visiting
Washington during Jefferson's administrations, described the
American capital as a place where

> Already has the child of Gallia's school
> The foul Philosophy that sins by rule
> . . . .
> Already has she pour'd her poison here.

He then pleasantly referred to French thought as garbage and
hinted that the president of the United States, obviously a
Unitarian or a deist and obviously therefore an infidel, slept
nightly in the arms of a black mistress.

Respectable Boston Unitarianism found itself in a difficult
position. It abhorred Jacobinism and voted the Federalist ticket.
But how could it avoid being tarred with the pitch of infidelity?
If it went back to trinitarian doctrine, it would not be Unitarian.
If it went forward, it would have no creed at all, cease to be a
religion, and risk being bracketed with French skepticism. In
Boston for a time conservative Unitarianism therefore did
nothing; hence the meaning of Emerson's stinging phrase that
from 1790 to 1820 there was not a book, a speech, a conversa-

tion, or a thought in Massachusetts. His judgment is more picturesque than sound.

The religious history of New England in the half-century that stretches from Lexington and Concord to the creation of the American Unitarian Association in 1825 is a strange, eventful history, nor can I do justice to its complexities. There were Old Light Calvinists and New Light Calvinists, Old Side Presbyterians and New Side Presbyterians, orthodox Unitarians, liberal Unitarians, Universalists, Baptists, Methodists, Roman Catholics, and other varieties of Christians in a commonwealth that at its founding had been content with the gospel according to the Rev. John Cotton. But the trend that interests us most is that represented by another entry in Emerson's journal in 1831: "I suppose it is not wise, not being natural, to belong to any religious party. In the bible you are not directed to be a Unitarian or a Calvinist or an Episcopalian."

What, then, were you directed to be? Not a hot-gospeller, preaching the fear of hell in picturesque but illiterate language; not an emotional exhorter like Lorenzo Dow, known as Crazy Dow; not even a revivalist like Charles Grandison Finney, who drove his hearers into physical convulsions and was charged with ruining the churches in western New York. Not this, surely; but was there no middle ground between the austerities of orthodox Unitarianism and the melodrama of religious demagoguery? Religion was of the highest spirituality; could it find no emotional expression satisfactory to sensitive and cultivated spirits other than the graceful formularies of the Episcopal church? Surely religion was an experience above, not beneath, the rational faculty. Or did the rational faculty require revaluation?

Liberal Unitarianism was a gradual development. Three or four significant steps can be listed. In 1803, the year of Emerson's birth, William Ellery Channing was inducted into the pastorate of the Federal Street Church in Boston, where he developed his views slowly and honestly. In 1815 he was compelled to refute a charge that he recognized nothing divine in the nature of Jesus, a refutation the more necessary, he thought, because he wished to differentiate liberal Unitarianism in America from the extreme rationalist position of Unitarianism in England. He asserted that

Jesus Christ is the only master of Christians, and whatever he taught, either during his personal ministry, or by his inspired Apostles, we regard as of divine authority, and profess to make the rule of our lives.

This was cautious enough, but in 1819 at the ordination of the Rev. Jared Sparks in Baltimore he went further and laid the groundwork for the formal liberal Unitarian creed, and, incidentally, for Emerson. The Scriptures, said Channing, were written by men for men at particular times and must be interpreted by the normal exercise of reason. If, as the Calvinist argues, man's reason is so dreadfully darkened by Adam's fall that its most decisive judgments are unworthy of trust, then not merely Christianity but natural theology also must be abandoned. If trinitarianism is true, we must infer that Christ came to change God's mind rather than the minds of men and that the highest object of his mission was to avert punishment rather than to communicate holiness. Trinitarianism, in Channing's view, rests upon a false philosophy, upon a corruption of Scripture that disfigures the teaching of Jesus. And he sternly indicted old-line Calvinism in passages like this:

We object . . . to that system, which arrogates to itself the name of Orthodoxy, and which is now industriously propagated through our country. According to its old and genuine forms, it teaches that God brings us into life wholly depraved, so that under the innocent features of our childhood is hidden a nature averse to all good and propense to all evil; a nature which exposes us to God's displeasure and wrath, even before we have acquired power to understand our duties, or to reflect upon our actions. . . . we come from the hands of our Maker, with such a constitution, and are placed under such influences and circumstances, as to render certain and infallible the total depravity of every human being, from the first moment of his moral agency, and it also teaches, that the offence of the child, who brings into life the ceaseless tendency to unmingled crime, exposes him to the sentence of everlasting damnation. . . . This system also teaches, that God selects from this corrupt mass a number to be saved, and plucks them by a special influence, from the common ruin; that the rest of mankind, though left without that special grace, which their conversion requires, are commanded to repent, under penalty of aggravated woe; and that forgiveness is promised them, on terms which their very constitution disposes them to reject, and in rejecting which they awfully enhance the punishments of hell.

With such a view of God, man, and the universe Channing would have nothing to do.

Channing's denial of Calvinistic pessimism fitted well into the rising prosperity of America after the War of 1812. It was also acceptable to many among the elite, particularly in Boston. By the late twenties liberal Unitarianism of the Channing sort was making inroads upon trinitarianism in seaboard cities of the Atlantic coast and in the so-called New England belt west of the Hudson; and by 1825 Channing was instrumental in founding the American Unitarian Association. At Harvard, to the scandal of conservatives, Henry Ware, a Unitarian, had already been made Hollis Professor of Divinity, and by 1819 Harvard College had formally recognized the faculty in theology as a separate entity within the structure of the university.

But Channing, remarkable man that he was, was no such profound scholar as Theodore Parker. All he was doing was, in a sense, to turn their own weapons of rational analysis against the Old Light Calvinists. He was on the whole content with the rational faculty of Locke. "To confide in God," he said, "we must first confide in the faculties by which He is apprehended and the proofs of His existence are weighed," and Channing assumed as a matter of course that a special revelation had been made through Jesus Christ, however you defined his nature, at a particular time in history and that this revelation is recorded in the Bible.

At first young Emerson was inclined to depart no further from orthodoxy than Channing had done. His early sermons are mostly standard liberal Unitarian doctrine. Eight of them concern "The Authority of Jesus," and of these eight he preached one more than fifty times. One can, by looking carefully through these early manuscripts, find hints at the revolution in thought Emerson was to proclaim, but if all we had of Emerson were the 170 sermons of his youth, we would probably conclude that he was only a younger and lesser Channing.

III

But a break came in the tradition of liberal Unitarianism. The grounds of Emerson's dissent from that faith are only dimly evident in an early sermon, "A Feast of Remembrance," which hints at his dissatisfaction with the ritual of the Lord's Supper as administered at the Second Church in Boston. This dissatisfaction increased until, as all the world knows, he resigned his pastorate in 1832 over this very issue. The death of his first wife, his own illness, various disasters in his family, his trip to Europe in 1832–33, notable for the beginning of a long friendship with Carlyle, his enormous reading, his distrust of the complacency of mercantile culture in Boston—all these matters forced him to confront the issues of life and death, of good and evil, of the relation of God to man and of man to God as a personal rather than as a merely theoretical problem. They also thrust him opportunely into the larger world of nineteenth-century thought, scientific, philosophical, and aesthetic, in the brilliant decade of the thirties. Europe was in ferment. All the eighteenth-century absolutes were breaking down. It was the age of the Revolution of July that drove out the Bourbons and substituted Louis Philippe, the Citizen King; the decade of the First Reform Bill in Britain; an age when the deaths of Scott and Goethe cleared the way for a new literary generation—writers like Carlyle and J. S. Mill, Balzac and George Sand; when the mechanical concept of the universe was yielding to a dynamic one; when astonishing inventions were remaking industry and transportation, and astonishing discoveries were remolding science; the age of Jackson and of communal utopianism; the age when Great Britain abolished slavery in all its possessions and there was even hope that in Russia the czar would free the serfs. It was, in short, an age of hope—what Emerson called the "Newness." "New occasions teach new duties," wrote James Russell Lowell. "Time makes ancient good uncouth." Why should theology not also experience renovation?

After long meditation Emerson abandoned the faculty psychology of Locke and the formal theology of the Harvard Divinity School. Why should not we also enjoy an original relation to the universe? Why should not we have a poetry and philosophy of insight and not of tradition, a religion by revelation to us, not a mere record of revelation to a dead and vanished generation? To establish this view he had, like Channing, to abandon the divinity of Christ as a special phenomenon, but he went beyond Channing and abandoned formal theology altogether. In perhaps the finest paragraph he ever wrote, one published at the end of his essay on "Illusion" in *The Conduct of Life* of 1860, he stated a principle of the immediacy of the individual soul to the divine order of the universe, and from this principle, once he had earlier accepted it, he never departed:

There is no chance and no anarchy in the universe. All is system and gradation. Every god is there sitting in his sphere. The young mortal enters the hall of the firmament; there is he alone with them alone, they pouring on him benedictions and gifts, and beckoning him up to their thrones. On the instant, and incessantly, fall snow-storms of illusions. He fancies himself in a vast crowd which sways this way and that and whose movement and doings he must obey; he fancies himself poor, orphaned, insignificant. The mad crowd drives hither and thither, now furiously commanding this thing to be done, now that. What is he that he should resist their will, and think or act for himself? Every moment new changes and new showers of deceptions to baffle and distract him. And when, by and by, for an instant, the air clears and the cloud lifts a little, there are the gods still sitting around him on their thrones,—they alone with him alone.

This was vision, not theology, metaphor rather than statement. Vision or metaphor, it is, however, the central theme in Emerson, the only differentiation between the book *Nature* of 1836, and his later affirmations being the trying out of new ways by which to relate man's finite experience to this splendid, infinite central power. The original motto to *Nature* had been a sentence out of Plotinus to the effect that nature is only the image or imitation of wisdom, but the 1847 edition replaces this with six lines by Emerson himself, concluding:

> And, striving to be man, the worm
> Mounts through all the spires of form.

It is idle for the logician to point out that mounting through an ascending series of forms is a process in time whereas the realization of loneness in the presence of deity is confrontation in an eternal Now. Logic and time are, for the transcendentalist, illusions.

To maintain this vision of an eternal Now in which the soul participates Emerson destroys, or rather imprisons, the faculty of reason according to John Locke. Reason, or common sense, or, as Emerson calls it, the understanding, which assumes there is nothing in the mind that was not previously in the senses, is all very well in its way. It will enable you to earn money, avoid being run over, converse on practical problems with your neighbor. It lets you deal with the world of things as they are, as so many commodities to be bought and sold, and even, in the material world, permits you to make those permutations and combinations of things and elements into new patterns we call inventions that are useful to man. Mix the wit of man with the principles of physics and the result is, for example, the railroad, or, as Emerson picturesquely says:

To diminish friction [man] paves the road with iron bars, and, mounting a coach with a shipload of men, animals, and merchandise behind him, he darts through the country, from town to town, like an eagle or a swallow through the air.

Emerson has been called an enraptured Yankee. The Yankee in him approves this utility in the inventive mind. The same quality in this writer leads him to disapprove of Brook Farm because he knows it won't work, and to engage Thoreau as his hired man because he knows Thoreau will work.

Emerson is always talking about polarities. The world for him has two handles. If you pick it up by the practical handle, if you look only through the eyes of the Yankee in Emerson, you look through the eyes of the man who served as Carlyle's literary agent, bought real estate in Concord, and gave young Americans a great deal of sound advice on how to get on in the world. But this is not Emerson the transcendentalist.

What does Emerson the transcendentalist believe? In the first place Emerson parallels German metaphysical thought by asserting that practical good sense, or what he calls the understanding, is not all of man's intellect. It is not even the highest quality in the mind. The human animal is more than an improved species of beast. Man is in fact set apart from the rest of nature by spirit, or, more accurately, by the consciousness of spirit. Emerson's attribution of spirit to the individual is, however, not quite identical with the theological attribution of a soul to man. In Emerson's eyes the notion of the soul as a separate and indestructible entity created at some indefinite period before the birth of a human being, joined with it at birth, and after the death of the body moving into some timeless state of happiness or pain—this for him is insufficient. Instead, his view is strongly tinged with Oriental ideas of the soul as simultaneously apart from, yet within, the divine nature of God. Soul or spirit in the human being has its phenomenal individuality and is in time to be distinguished from the timeless, spaceless, and immaterial existence that is the ground of all being. Why is it thus momentarily separated from essential and universal being Emerson never quite makes clear, but he accepts this separateness as a fact in experience.

By reason of this separateness, spirit in man can be dulled by use and wont in the material world, by an over-concern for low issues and vulgar aims, by the wrong kind of passivity, but the separatism is never absolute and may at any moment be transcended. Man can consciously or unconsciously open himself to an influx from God, or essential being. Such an opening of the individuality to God is not necessarily an act of consciousness, for it may come unbidden. Emerson records such an experience:

Crossing a bare common, in snow puddles, at twilight, under a clouded sky, without having in my thoughts any occurrence of special good fortune I have enjoyed a perfect exhilaration. I am glad to the brink of fear.

The channel of this influx, the way by which man may intuit his relation to the quintessence of being—this Emerson calls the Reason, a word he spells with a capital letter. Reason is for him not a logical process but rather the capacity of the spirit in man to grasp immediately truths that lie beyond ordinary logic and common sense and that are also the ground of being of the world of common sense in space and time. Reason for Emerson is only partially the Vernunft of Kant; he adds to the concept of Reason an important component of vision.

Inasmuch as the capacity thus to lie open to the inflowing of divinity or the essence of being is forever a fact of life, any unique revelation at some particular time and place to some particular person or persons is, if it pretend to be unique, essentially misleading. History records a number of such experiences and records that of Christ as being one among many. Even though the teaching of Christ comes closest to being the perfect teaching, Emerson held that equally valid intuitions of divine meaning were possible to him in Concord and are possible anywhere at any time to anybody. If I may parody John Stuart Mill, Emerson argues for a perpetual possibility of revelation; and this perpetual possibility is evidence of what is godlike in mortality.

What we call evil is the blindness of man to such potentialities. As it is sometimes said that Emerson is oblivious to sin, pain, and evil, I must point out that for him evil exists and is privative —it is being blind to such infinite potentialities. This of course scarcely deals with the problem of pain but it does squarely front the twin problems of sin and evil. That blindness, which we think of as sin or evil, may originate in a variety of ways; and it must be confessed that Emerson never thoroughly explores the origins of evil, nor did he quite explain how the power of evil is somehow ended by a sudden influx of divinity. It is, however, one thing to ignore evil and quite another thing to say that you do not know how evil originates or to deny that evil is one of the primary facts of life, something Emerson never did. Moreover, in the Christian system evil or sin is diminished or erased by a mysterious psychological revolution called conversion, and it would, I think, be difficult to show that Emerson is somehow less explicit in this regard than is Christian dogma.

Regarding the nature of the spiritual existence that creates and underlies the world as we know it and that can flood the soul in unpredictable moments Emerson is again not quite explicit. Perhaps no mystic can ever put his ineffable vision into words. Negatively one can say that Emerson's God is not the God of trinitarian theology, nor, indeed, the Christian deity of any standard formulary of Christian theology. Indeed, Emerson's struggle to define the relation of God and the soul frequently carries him into expressions that from the point of view of conservative Christian orthodoxy border on blasphemy. And he is inconsistent in his use of terms. Sometimes God is the Over-Soul—that is, the absolute spirit that timelessly maintains the universe and man. Sometimes God seems to be an absolute system of Platonic ideas. Sometimes God is shrouded in pantheism, and sometimes He is an immanent presence. Sometimes Emerson even goes so far as to imply that God and man, or at least man in his highest potentiality, are virtually one. This is less shocking when one realizes that if God was incarnate in

63

Jesus, and if in Emerson's view Christ was merely man as he ought to be and might become, any man approaching this ideal existence became by so much like God or became God. "The soul," Emerson writes, "knows no persons. It invites every man to expand to the full circle of the universe, and will have no preferences but those of spontaneous love." He makes the remarkable assertion that "the soul gives itself, alone, original and pure, to the Lonely, Original and Pure, who, on that condition, gladly inhabits, leads, and speaks through it." Man becomes God. But is it not thus in all ages that mystics have tried to describe the indescribable?

Concerning the great triangle of the soul, God, and nature, Emerson holds that nature is at once a barrier between man and God, a conduit through which the divine flows into man, and evidence of the immutable principles of all being. The visible world is to the commonplace mind an end in itself. At its lowest and meanest level it sustains life as biology, life as commerce, life as politics; and though even to the commonplace mind the life of material nature is regulated by uniform law and that law reveals hints of beauty and is the foundation of language, most men are not yet sufficiently wise to translate the usefulness of nature and the uniformity of its behavior into higher principles.

Yet mechanical principles do not operate of themselves. Nor are they in themselves visible; all that we can see is the phenomenal manifestation of invisible principles or powers at work in matter. But if the invisibility of laws regulating the phenomenal world be thus granted, to what source can we attribute these mysterious and secret forces? To something phenomenal and concrete, or to something as invisible and immaterial as the mysterious power of gravitation or the equally mysterious principle that we cannot experience the world except through time and space? What if these essential, yet invisible principles are themselves as inferior to their invisible origin as the phenomenal world is inferior to them? Is it not also conceivable that great moral principles, also invisible, are like the unseen forces that keep the stars in their courses and manage life, growth, and death? That there are great moral principles all men assume, however they may differ about the expression of their existence. And as all lines meet in infinity or God, so it is possible that all general principles, whether in ethics or in chemistry, meet in the divine. A nobly phrased passage toward the end of Emerson's little book on *Nature* sums up this part of his teaching:

The world proceeds from the same spirit as the body of man. It is a remoter and inferior incarnation of God, a projection of God in the unconscious. But it differs from the body in one important respect. It is not, like that, now subjected to the human will. Its serene order is inviolable by us. It is, therefore, to us the present expositor of the divine mind.

Aside from the objections that can be raised against any form of philosophical idealism, Emersonian transcendentalism faces, it seems to me, two fundamental difficulties. The first I have already hinted. Man is a being in nature and simultaneously a being in God. Insofar as for Emerson nature is phenomenal rather than noumenal—that is, a system of objects other than ideas and principles invisible to mortality and evident to the Reason only—man, still a member of the animal kingdom though possessing that portion of divinity one calls his soul, lives in the world of the understanding, subjected to its laws, and unable except at random moments to transcend his ordinary sensory being. Except to the eye of faith he is born, lives, and dies like any other being in the universe of time and space. Yet he simultaneously lives, though he may be aware of this only fitfully (or in the worst case never know it at all), in the timeless order of infinity—in an eternal Now. How can he be in both universes of discourse simultaneously?

It is important to realize that with all his talk about a divine influx flooding the soul and making it aware of its eternal relations, Emerson tacitly assumes that the soul in question is that of an adult. He nowhere explicitly takes the view of Wordsworth in the great "Ode on the Intimations of Immortality Recollected from Early Childhood" that the infant, the child, the adolescent is competent to pass in moments of illumination from the world of the understanding to the universe of Reason or intuition. Even in the beautiful "Threnody," written on the death of his son, Emerson does not attribute to the dead hyacinthine boy, for whom

Morn well might break and April bloom,

any special insight into the divine order of which he was a signal and a type. In short, the time process governs the lives of men; it notably governs their lives until they reach maturity. And at the other end of the temporal spectrum we grow old and die. But there is no senility in Emerson's scheme though, by a sad irony, he himself sank into aphasia and never completed his "History of the Intellect" which he dreamed might have cleared his system, if system it can be called, of discordancies and ambiguities.

Emerson is in the curious difficulty of postulating man as living simultaneously in time and in eternity, whereas in most religions man is born into time and dies into eternity. His difficulty can conceivably be met, but it cannot be argued that he makes clear how random moments of insight transfer man as a temporal being into a semblance or replica of God while he still exists in a world of time and space. In one sense this is of course

66

the difficulty of all mysticism; in another sense, given Emerson's practical grasp upon the world of things as they are, it is surprising that he never faced his central dilemma: for him man remains an infinite being only randomly conscious of his infinite nature. As for the doctrine of the immortality of the soul Emerson of course thinks that man, the infinite being, is immortal, but he says very little about the continuity of personality in an afterlife, which is for most believers what is meant by immortality.

The second major difficulty, however, he really struggled to overcome, though whether he solved the dilemma is matter for argument. His original formula postulated a universe more or less in being rather than a universe in the process of becoming. Born into an apparent time-space, man in moments of illumination, whether through his will or through his unconscious, can unite himself with the timeless; that is, he breaks through the static pattern of this world into the world of the eternal and the divine. Always interested in science, Emerson was uncomfortably aware, if not of evolution in the Darwinian sense, then of development and change in the pre-Darwinian phases of evolutionary doctrine—hence the change of motto for his *Nature* from a statement by Plotinus about being, to a statement by Emerson about becoming. But if man is subjected to some sort of development or evolutionary growth, how is this to be equated with his potential and immediate participation in an absolute spiritual order? At what stage in its development does the race become capable of a competent intuition of the divine? As Henry David Gray has pointed out, in a developmental world it is not sufficient to think of the soul as an emanation of deity. Man cannot *belong* to one kind of existence—that of evolution—and also *be* in another—the world of absolute idealism. For if one postulates

67

a developmental scheme of things and simultaneously postulates an intuitional access to absolute being, we have to answer either or both of two questions: at what stage does the individual become competent to intuit deity; and at what stage does the race thus become competent? Is access to the transcendental vision equally possible to an Australian bushman, a Digger Indian, an African pygmy, and a cultivated Unitarian clergyman? And will they each intuit the same vision of the absolute? It will not quite do to say that the expression of idealistic faith is possible in all cultures, being differently expressed in different times and places, for the point is not the relativity of the expression but the locus of the line that separates man from the animal kingdom and, separating him, permits him to climb through all the spires of form into spiritual maturity.

Emerson recognized the difficulty. He tried to argue that man is related to the evolving world of matter by his form, and to the absolute world of being by his spirit. He seemed on occasion to hint what Whitman was more richly to affirm, that even the worm may enjoy some sort of higher sympathy and that this sympathy develops in man to the highest level of religious ecstasy. But the argument is not wholly convincing. Are there grades in absolute being, some accessible to the worm and others accessible to Emerson? The interesting question arises, one which commentators on Emerson never wholly solve, whether the central principle in the Emersonian universe is pure spirit or some sort of vitalism commoner in nineteenth-century scientific speculation than it seems to be today.

I trust I have not dwelt unduly upon some of the inconsistencies in a writer who never set out to be consistent and who, in fact, in one celebrated passage, repudiated consistency as a hobgoblin to little minds. I do not wish to derogate from Emerson's greatness. It is probable that no greater number of flaws can be found in his reading of life than can be found in the thought of far more systematic professional philosophers. It is fatally easy to find logical contradictions in Emerson. But the insight of the poet is sometimes worth more than the syllogisms of the metaphysician. In 1865, says Clarence Gohdes in his book on the *Periodicals of American Transcendentalism*, a student at Williams College sought out Emerson for an interview and asked him what transcendentalism truly is. Emerson replied:

If we will only see that which is about us, we shall see also above. Is God far from any of us? There is an equality of the human spirit to the world's phenomena. We look neither up to the universe nor down to it, but confront it. . . . The Transcendentalist sees everything as idealist. That is, all events, objects, etc., seen, are images to the consciousness. It is the thought of them only that one sees. You shall find God in the unchanged essence of the universe, the air, the river, the leaf; and in the subjective unfolding of your nature, the determination of the private spirit, everything of religion.[2]

Perhaps this is as close as Emerson could come to a simple statement of his faith in man, God, and the universe.

[2] Clarence L. F. Gohdes, *The Periodicals of American Transcendentalism* (Durham, N.C., 1931), pp. 4–5.

·» IV «·

THE COSMIC OPTIMISM OF
WALT WHITMAN

I

L̲IKE OTHER SORTS of historians, students of religion in America, particularly of American Protestantism, cannot avoid being attracted to dramatic event and picturesque personality. The clash of theological systems, conflicts among church leaders, clerical scandals, the struggles between liberals and conservatives, the rise of new religions (particularly if their creation can be traced to individuals of great psychological interest), the impact of secular ideas upon theological tenets—these are persons and conflicts the historian can dramatize. How else account for the twenty-one varieties of Methodists in the United States, the twenty-nine species of Baptists, the rise of Mormonism, Spiritualism, and Christian Science? Henry Ward Beecher, a specious orator and shallow thinker, for this reason gets a vast deal of attention; quiet and influential theologians or scholars like Nathaniel Emmons and George Foot Moore get much less. Religious history takes on a dramatic, sometimes even a melodramatic, tone; an episode like the Andover heresy trials of 1886 is given a prominence in the religious story far out of proportion to its influence upon American life.

Whatever the bitternesses engendered by religious disputes, imaginative writers in America have, on the other hand, shown an indisposition to become involved in sectarian warfare. During the French Revoluton, it is true, writers were frequently judged by their adherence to conservative or radical philosophies and frequently wrote with these philosophies as premises for poem and novel. During the nineteenth century it is also true that the American fiction has sometimes taken the problem of belief and disbelief for one of its themes. Two examples are Mrs. Stowe's *The Minister's Wooing* and Harold Frederic's *The Damnation of Theron Ware*. In these books the insufficiency of theological dogma or the cultural vulgarity engendered by orthodoxy of a narrow sort is explicitly or implicitly condemned. Few novelists, however, have made the tenets of a particular church an affirmative theme; most novelists tend to assume that humanity, or, as some would say, the human heart, is paramount and that a mere set of theological articles is inadequate as a guide of life unless it be richly interpreted in the spirit of humanity. Two great examples are Hawthorne's *The Scarlet Letter* and Mrs. Stowe's *Uncle Tom's Cabin*. Most of the religious novels I have looked into make their subject the education by life of a minister or a partisan of some form of Christian orthodoxy into a wider knowledge of, and sympathy for, his fellow men. There are, doubtless, stories of a contrary tendency; in general, however, American fictionists tend to the view that sectarianism is a blind alley. It should be said, even if parenthetically, that atheism as a pattern of systematic value judgments is seldom a positive force in American writing. Even the agnostic Theodore Dreiser, with all his chemisms and his determinism, ends his career with *The Stoic*, a novel of mysticism. And a book like *The Octopus* of Frank

Norris includes as a major component of the tale the mystical visions into which Vanamee falls.

Imaginative American literature since the French Revolution has had, then, an irenic purpose not commonly recognized. It has sought a kind of Protestant ecumenicism. To this general statement there are of course one or two large exceptions. The struggle over slavery broke most of the Protestant churches into hostile factions, and as controversy grew, charges of religious hypocrisy were made by each side against the other. Thus Whittier, whom we commonly think of as a peaceful Quaker bard, in a poem like "A Sabbath Scene" harshly portrays a slave-owning minister in church calling on his congregation to arrest a shrieking female slave; and in another poem, "The Haschisch," argues that pro-slavery sentiment acted like a drug on Protestant ministers. Southern writers in turn denounced Northern pastors as narrow and unbiblical.

A second reservation must be made about the treatment of Catholicism by many of the standard American authors of the nineteenth century. Oliver Wendell Holmes declared that Boston, the city of three hills, would conquer Rome, the city of seven hills; and Whittier in a poem of 1851 could refer unpleasantly to "Rome's harlot triple-crowned." Two years later, in some verses on official piety, he described the Roman church as

> Listening at her altars to the cry
> Of midnight Murder, while her hounds of hell
> Scour France, from baptized cannon and holy bell
> And thousand-throated priesthood, loud and high,
> Pealing Te Deums to the shuddering sky.

Mark Twain's *Innocents Abroad* is full of jibes at Roman Catholic practices, and Charles Eliot Norton's *Notes of Travel and*

Study in Italy is not distinguished by charity toward that church. But though American Victorians could not always escape from traditional denunciation of the Scarlet Woman of Babylon, the general religious movement in literature was, as I have said, a movement in the direction of ecumenicism embracing Protestantism as a whole and in the case of a poet like Longfellow including Catholicism and Judaism as well.

Of course Emerson transcended all formal religions. Whitman I shall come to in a moment. Despite severe limits to Whittier's tolerance, that poet so far follows Quaker tradition that his characteristic religious poems, some of them still sung in Protestant churches, proclaim a doctrine of universal love. The best known is "The Eternal Goodness" of 1867. The poem deprecates sectarian quarrels, and a famous stanza proclaims eternal love:

> I know not where His islands lift
> Their fronded palms in air;
> I only know I cannot drift
> Beyond His love and care.

Whittier was certainly more liberal in outlook than Lowell, who, though he was touched in youth by transcendentalism and though his great "Commemoration Ode" is a plea for reconciliation between the sections, was too bound by Brahmin parochialism, Anglo-Saxon racism, the fear of evolution, and straight-out anti-Semitism to write in favor of universal brotherhood. Of all the great New Englanders he strikes me as the most provincial in this respect.

The same cannot be said of Oliver Wendell Holmes, commonly regarded as Bostonianism incarnate. Holmes struggled to equate modern medicine, modern astronomy, and the evolutionary philosophy with the traditional doctrine of design or final

73

causes in the universe as evidence of deity; his distrust of Roman Catholicism was not violent; and he denounced sectarianism and pleaded for a universal doctrine of Christian love, as in the concluding lines of his long meditative poem, "Wind-Clouds and Star-Drifts":

> Not from the sad-eyed hermit's lonely cell,
> Not from the conclave where the holy men
> Glare on each other, as with angry eyes
> They battle for God's glory and their own,
> Till, sick of wordy strife, a show of hands
> Fixes the faith of ages yet unborn,—
> Ah, not from these the listening soul can hear
> The Father's voice that speaks itself divine!
> Love must be still our Master! till we learn
> What He can teach us of a woman's heart,
> We know not Him whose love embraces all.

This first appeared in *The Poet at the Breakfast-Table* serialized in the *Atlantic Monthly* in 1871–72. Some two years earlier Holmes had reworked a poem called "At the Pantomime," rebuking himself and others for anti-Semitism. Seeing a group of Jews in a theater, including a young boy, Holmes blushed for his prejudice against them. The poem ends:

> Thy prophets caught the Spirit's flame,
> From thee the Son of Mary came,
> With thee the Father deigned to dwell,—
> Peace be upon thee, Israel!

But the true proponent of Protestant ecumenicism in America—indeed, the proponent of ecumenicism in the widest sense—was Henry Wadsworth Longfellow, a writer whose important contributions to religious tolerance have never been rightly evaluated. A formal Unitarian, Longfellow rose above all creeds to denounce religious fanaticism as in the "Torquemada" of *Tales of the Wayside Inn,* and Puritan cruelty as in the two *New*

England Tragedies that conclude his ambitious *The Divine Tragedy*. No one, said Ruskin, entered more sympathetically into the life of the medieval monk than did Longfellow; and Robert Frost was fond of reciting the perfect little medieval mystery play to be found in Longfellow's *The Golden Legend* and teasing his friends to identify it. It must also be remembered that this son of New England translated Dante's *Divine Comedy* and in so doing created one of the great translations in American literature. There are weaknesses in Longfellow; what moderns overlook is that he sought to infuse the bleakness of Protestant culture with the human warmth and emotional color of the Roman Catholic tradition. Moreover, among the storytellers in *Tales of the Wayside Inn* is Isaac Edrahi, the Spanish Jew into whose mouth are put wonderful versions of Jewish lore, as, for example, "The Legend of Rabbi Ben Levin." The Talmud gave Longfellow one of his greatest religious lyrics, "Sandalphon":

> Have you read in the Talmud of old,
> In the legends that Rabbins have told
>   Of the limitless realms of the air,
> Have you read it,—the marvellous story
> Of Sandalphon, the Angel of Glory,
>   Sandalphon, the Angel of Prayer?
>
> . . . .
>
> . . . serene in the rapturous throng
> Unmoved by the rush of the song,
>   With eyes unimpassioned and slow,
> Among the dead angels, the deathless
> Sandalphon stands listening breathless
>
>   To sounds that ascend from below;—
> From the spirits on earth that adore,
> From the souls that entreat and implore
>   In the fervor and passion of prayer;
>
> . . . .

75

And he gathers the prayers as he stands,
And they change into flowers in his hands,
Into garlands of purple and red;
And beneath the great arch of the portal,
Through the streets of the City Immortal
Is wafted the fragrance they shed.

Successful or not, Longfellow's long trilogy, *The Divine Tragedy*, presenting in dramatic form ancient, medieval, and modern Christianity, is set in a philosophic framework that postulates the eventual overcoming of evil by compassion—the *Caritas* of Christian theology. The last speech in this enormous work is a soliloquy by St. John, the Beloved Apostle. Here is part of it:

The portals of Time unfold
On hinges of iron, that grate
And groan with the rust and the weight,
Like the hinges of a gate
That hath fallen to decay;
But the evil doth not cease;
There is war instead of peace,
Instead of Love there is hate;
And still I must wander and wait,
Still I must watch and pray.

. . . .

From all vain pomps and shows,
From the pride that overflows,
And the false conceit of men;
Bewildered in its search,

. . . .

Bewildered with the cry:
Lo here! lo there, the Church!
Poor sad Humanity
Through all the dust and heat
Turns back with bleeding feet,
By the weary road it came,
Unto the simple thought

By the great Master taught,
And that remaineth still:
Not he that repeateth the name
But he that doeth the will!

I think it is clear that the movement among imaginative writers toward ecumenicism emphasized the fatherhood of God.

One of the operative words in the soliloquy I have just quoted is "Humanity"—"poor sad Humanity," writes Longfellow. The sympathy for humanity lambent in Longfellow's pages reflects an earlier fire kindled in Europe—the religion of humanity, the belief in Man with a capital M.

In 1830 the age of reaction seemed to have ended; it was, as all good liberals believed, to be replaced by the age of the religion of humanity, a concept at once powerful and vague, exciting and illogical. This gentler child of the French Revolution was to be all powerful for the future of mankind. The gigantic talent of Jules Michelet, unleashed by the Revolution of July, produced, beginning in 1833, his vast *Histoire de France*, a work he felt himself competent to write, not because he had the training of a specialist but because, the child of the people, he understood instinctively that the French people were France. The equally gigantic talent of Victor Hugo produced plays, poetry, and prose hymning the social outcast and the common man, a hymn that reached its climax in the Promethean figure of Jean Valjean, the hero of *Les Miserables*, in 1862. Hugo's prolific contemporary, George Sand, not only edited her weekly paper, *La Cause du Peuple*, in 1848, but wrote novels like *Le Compagnon du Tour de France*, in which a Christlike carpenter, a workingman, becomes ideal man. In Dickens and Bulwer-Lytton Britain contributed its vindications of the poor or of social uplift. Since Dickens is the more familiar nowadays, I mention *A Christmas*

77

Carol, The Chimes, and *The Cricket on the Hearth* among the Christmas stories, and, in the fifties and sixties, novels like *The Old Curiosity Shop, Dombey and Son, Bleak House,* and *Little Dorrit,* tales in which to be outcast is to be divine, to be imprisoned is to challenge altruism, and to be poor is to love mankind. In Germany, meanwhile, Heinrich Heine attacked the church, monarchy, the aristocracy, and the police in the name of a mystic entity called Germany; and in Russia Turgenev was in 1852 exiled to his estates for eulogizing Gogol. His books, beginning with *A Sportsman's Sketches* in 1852, urged the intellectuals to go among the people. Even opera was affected: such popular favorites as Rossini's *William Tell,* Bellini's *La Sonnambula,* and Donizetti's *Linda di Chamouni* were laid in Switzerland, the home of liberty. Aristocrats fare badly in Verdi's *Luisa Miller, Rigoletto, Il Trovatore,* and *La Traviata.* In Bellini's *Norma* (1831) the Roman invader betrays true love; and what is the perennial *Lucia di Lammermoor* but the tale of the love of a poor man for a girl, betrayed by the treachery of the aristocratic rich?

And behind these works of art were vast, vague, powerful philosophic schemes for releasing the pent-up powers of the people for the salvation of mankind—Saint-Simonianism, Fourierism, the secular religion of humanity in August Comte, Proudhon's remarkable discovery that property is theft, the proclamation by Mazzini that "God exists because we exist; God lives in our conscience, in the conscience of humanity." There were even liberal ecclesiastical enthusiasts like Lamennais, who dreamed of turning the massive structure of Roman Catholicism into a democratic theocracy. The first issue of his liberal weekly, *L'Avenir,* which appeared in October, 1830, carried the famous slogan: "God and liberty." Alas, four years later, he left the church forever, signaling his departure by publishing his influential *Paroles d'un Croyant*, a book that had a world-wide vogue and that seemed to Pope Gregory XVI "immense in its perversity." Never before or since in the history of the Western world has a philosophy of democracy, the religion of humanity, been more enthusiastically proclaimed or supported with greater ardor than in the period from 1830 to 1850. We cannot understand Walt Whitman unless we understand that he drew upon the doctrine of the benevolence of God in this country and the doctrine of the religion of humanity abroad.

II

Those who cannot believe Shakespeare wrote his plays because nothing in his schooling prophesies *Hamlet* should consider Walt Whitman. He left school at the age of eleven or twelve. His family had no interest in literature and no understanding of his purpose. Among his eight brothers and sisters one brother remained a child all his life, one, who was syphilitic, went insane, one died a consumptive, one married a wife of dubious morality and was himself no model citizen, and one sister proved to be highly neurotic. Had Whitman died at the age of thirty-six, he would not now be remembered. He spent most of his life away from home, he drifted from job to job and enjoyed long periods of idleness, he was intermittently a local politician and a newspaper editor, he wrote bad verse, worse fiction, and merely competent editorials. Yet in 1855 because of some mysterious psychological alchemy we know nothing about, this lazy Long Islander underwent a fundamental transformation. He then printed the first version of one of the seminal books in American literature, *Leaves of Grass*, a title that sometimes means a particular book and sometimes all of his poetical production, a work he constantly revised and added to, not always to its advantage. He invented a new form of poetry and created a style uniquely his own. He somehow acquired a working knowledge of many branches of science and of pseudo-science, of operatic and choral music, of contemporary European thought and literature, a wide grasp of geography, an easy fund of historical information, a great range of acquaintances, and a sense of mission as an American writer unparalleled in earlier literature.

Our concern is with Whitman's religious views, but we must first note certain difficulties in ascertaining what they are. Like Poe, Whitman was three-fifths genius and two-fifths sheer fudge. He was capable of posing and pretentiousness. He was not a systematic thinker. He used words loosely and inconsistently. He passed through various phases of affirmation and depression, each of which left some trace upon his masterpiece. We shall probably never know the secret of his inner life. Though he was the first great celebrant of sex in American literature, we can discover nothing about his sexual experiences, but only that he never married, that he once boasted of having engendered illegitimate children, and that his passionate attachment to young men, most of them without culture, together with the warmth of his expression when he was celebrating what he called "adhesiveness," exposed him to a charge of homosexuality that never quite clears away. But he was also kindly, modest, generous, self-sacrificing, simple, and essentially good—altogether one of the most complex personalities in the nineteenth century.

The reader who comes upon Whitman for the first time discovers that the word which seems to recur most frequently in his poetry is the first personal pronoun; and we may begin by asking what Whitman means in his poems by the pronoun "I." One immediately faces a paradox. The "I" is the poet himself, but the poet seems to address his own soul as a being separate from himself. It has been suggested that his way of speaking both to and of the soul may be a habit lingering from Whitman's days as a newspaper editor, when the editorial "we" was one thing and the private individuality of the editor another. And there is something to this. Moreover, it is common in poetry for the writer as a private personality to invent a public personality, a mask through which he can speak without embarrassment sentiments or judgments appropriate to the poem. Such a mask is in modern criticism called a *persona*. Utterances through the *persona* are or may be entirely sincere but may differ from utterances in private correspondence or private speech. Part of our difficulty in understanding Shakespeare's *Sonnets* is that we have no clue by which to differentiate raw autobiographical matter from matter dramatically appropriate to any poem, the poet from the *persona*. Certainly there is something like this in Whitman.

But the differentiation in Whitman between the speaker addressing his soul and the soul speaking as another "I" goes a little beyond the familiar psychological pattern of the *persona*. Whitman seems to feel that he is one thing and his soul is another thing; and that Walt Whitman, a person in time, has a special relation to, and a special interest in, an ineffable individual also named Walt Whitman, who lives beyond time and space. "The soul," he writes in "Song of Prudence,"

> is of itself,
> All verges to it, all has reference to what ensues,
> All that a person does, says, thinks, is of consequence
> Not a move can a man or woman make, that affects
> him or her in a day, month, any part of the
> direct lifetime, or the hour of death,

> But the same affects him or her onward afterward
> through the indirect lifetime.

> The indirect is just as much as the direct,
> The spirit receives from the body just as much
> as it gives to the body, if not more.

"I am," he wrote in a famous line from "Song of Myself,"

> the poet of the Body and I am the poet of the Soul.

It is obviously right for the temporal Walt Whitman to address the immortal Walt Whitman, for the man living directly to speak to and of the soul indirectly; the difficulty is that in this respect as in others Whitman is inconsistent. All we can do is to note the distinction, sometimes clear and sometimes blurred, and pass on to a closer examination of the pronoun "I" in his poetry.

The "I" in *Leaves of Grass* may mean any one of four or five several existences or bundles of experience in time or in eternity.

In the first place *Leaves of Grass* is obviously autobiographical in the customary sense. Walt Whitman lived on fish-shaped Paumonok, Walt Whitman crossed on the Brooklyn ferry, Walt Whitman went to Washington and nursed soldiers, recording his memories, or some of them, in the poems entitled *Drum-Taps*, brought out in 1865. For the most part such passages are reliable, though when Whitman talks about the family in his poems, he is speaking through a *persona* and not directly, for the Whitman tribe was by no means as affectionate and unified as the family model in *Leaves of Grass* pictures it to be.

In the second place, if the actual Walt Whitman can, as he does, recall and record in his poem his experiences in Brooklyn or Manhattan, as a swimmer in Long Island Sound, as a carpenter building houses, and so on, there is no reason why he cannot imaginatively extend this range of experiences and memories and, as the moderns say, "identify" by extension with a number of other imagined activities, traversing regions he had never set foot in when he wrote particular passages, and imagining emotional experiences that he should or could have had but that perhaps never occurred. This again is nothing novel in imaginative writing, but in this shadowy region where fact and fancy interfuse, the riddle of Whitman's sexual history is hidden. No one has more beautifully described the ecstasy of perfect sexual union than has Whitman, but how much of it is remembered and how much is imagined biographers cannot tell.

But there is a third and higher level of significance for the letter "I" in Whitman. The intent of his poem is to celebrate America, the intent of the poet is to prefigure great national bards to come; and after 1855, but particularly after the Civil War and during the Gilded Age, Whitman had one great advantage and one great disadvantage in presenting the symbolic American to the world. The great advantage was of course the heroism of the boys who fought the Civil War; the disadvantage was the crass corruption of the Grant administrations. He had somehow to create a figure that would celebrate the one, and shroud the other, facet of democracy. He had to find a single great type of American that had been, and was, and was to be. Accordingly the "I" of the poem is also the nobler, multiple American of all time. Dilating the bard, as it were, into an enormous replica of Walt Whitman, he writes of himself as one simultaneously present in a thousand different places and participating in a thousand varied scenes. The long catalogues of types, scenes, and occupations in *Leaves of Grass*, impossible for a single person to experience, can be simultaneously felt only by such a type figure. This figure toils westward with the pioneers, fights on board the *Bonhomme Richard*, wanders southward with slave and planter, is convict and judge, prostitute and president, anybody and nobody. This "I" is the American Everyman.

He appears again and again in Whitman's pages. I select as a representative instance this passage from "Song of the Answerer," in which the American Everyman is momentarily translated from the first person to the third, a grammatical change that does not affect Whitman's fundamental concept:

> He says indifferently and alike *How are you friend?*
> to the President at his levee.
> And he says *Good-day my brother,* to Cudge that
> hoes in the sugar-field,
> And both understand him and know that his speech
> is right.
>
> He walks with perfect ease in the capitol,
> He walks among the Congress, and one Representa-
> tive says to another, *Here is our equal ap-
> pearing and new.*
>
> Then the mechanics take him for a mechanic,
> And the soldiers suppose him to be a soldier,
> and the sailors that he has follow'd the
> sea,
> And the authors take him for an author, and
> the artists for an artist,
> And the laborers perceive he could labor with
> them and love them,
> No matter what the nation, that he might find
> his brothers and sisters there.
>
> . . . .
>
> The gentleman of perfect blood acknowledges his
> perfect blood,
> The insulter, the prostitute, the angry person,
> the beggar, see themselves in the ways of
> him, he strongly transmutes them,
> They are not vile any more, they hardly know
> themselves they are so grown.

In this passage the general identification of the individual with everything American pushes beyond the boundaries of the United States and takes on international standing. This, too, is part of Whitman's intention, an aim the more determined as he saw the United States putting its worst foot forward in the Gilded Age. He wrote in "Years of the Modern":

> I see not America only, not only Liberty's
>   nation, but other nations preparing,
> I see tremendous entrances and exits, new combi-
>   nations, the solidarity of races,
> I see that force advancing with irresistible
>   power on the world's stage,
>
> . . . .
>
> I see Freedom, completely arm'd and victorious
>   and very haughty, with Law on one side
>   and Peace on the other,
> A stupendous trio all issuing forth against the
>   idea of caste;
> What historic denouements are these we so
>   rapidly approach?

In sum, the universal American "I" is generalized into the universal "I" of the religion of humanity, since the inevitable outcome of history becomes the spread of democracy. The coming of the first Japanese mission to the United States in 1858 occasioned Whitman's poem "A Broadway Pageant," and the completion of the Suez Canal and the Union Pacific Railroad in 1869 suggested his masterly "Passage to India" of 1871. "Passage to India," which begins as a survey of the globe, a statement of comparative religion, and an examination of world history, is not content to remain on earth but soars more and more into the illimitable. Here, for example is such a section:

> O we can wait no longer,
> We too take ship O Soul,

Joyous we too launch out on trackless seas,
Fearless for unknown shores on waves of ecstasy
    to sail,
Amid the wafting winds, (thou pressing me to thee,
    I thee to me, O soul,)
Caroling free, singing our song of God,
Chanting our chant of pleasant exploration.

With laugh and many a kiss,
(Let others deprecate, let others weep for sin,
    remorse, humiliation,)
O soul thou pleasest me, I thee.

Ah more than any priest O Soul we too believe
    in God,
But with the mystery of God we dare not dally.

And, a little later:

> Greater than stars or suns,
> Bounding O Soul thou journeyest forth;
> What love than thine and ours could wider am-
>   plify?
> What aspirations, wishes, outvie thine and ours
>   O soul?
> What dreams of the ideal? What plans of puri-
>   ty, perfection, strength?
>
> .   .   .   .
>
> Reckoning ahead O soul, when thou, the time
>   achiev'd
> The seas all cross'd, weather'd the capes, the
>   voyage done,
> Surrounded, copest, frontest God, yieldest, the
>   aim attain'd,
> As filled with friendship, love complete, the
>   Elder Brother found,
> The Younger melts in fondness in his arms.

As I earlier said, Whitman in this passage addresses his own
soul as an entity separate from, yet identical with, Walt Whitman. But the soul has now soared above politics and history, and

has become the transcendental and timeless and indestructible entity of most mystical religions. It is significant, I think, that in this passage God does not figure as a Father but as an Elder Brother, who receives his Younger Brother, the human soul, after its passage through time into eternity.

III

Since for Whitman all existence in any sense of the word means intensely and means well—virtue, crime, genius, idiocy, men, women, children, all of what used to be known as animated nature, the geological ages, history in the largest sense, the universe itself—it follows in the main that what we call evil is merely a conventional judgment. To the mortal eye men are evil by inheritance, environment, temperament, opportunity, but evil is not, as with Emerson, even privative, it is, on the contrary, a positive, not a negative, component of society and the soul. Evil is, so to speak, merely one chord in an ever ascending symphony, a mere passing note, to change the figure, in the vast, affirmative composition, lyric and intense, we call Being. But there is one aspect of evil, or at least what commonly passes for evil, that requires special consideration, and that is death. In a real sense Whitman is the great poet of death.

What about this great enigma? It haunts *Leaves of Grass* in all its editions and all its phases. It is not only the theme of "When Lilacs Last in the Dooryard Bloomed," it appears over and over again in *Drum-Taps*, it is the occasion of so inferior a poem as "A Voice from Death," written about the Johnstown flood of 1889, and it is interwoven into the fabric of one of his greatest poems, "Out of the Cradle Endlessly Rocking." In "Song of Myself" one finds a passage like this concerning the dead:

> They are alive and well somewhere,
> The smallest sprout shows there is really no
>   death,
> And if ever there was it led forward life, and
>   does not wait at the end to arrest it,
> And ceas'd the moment life appear'd.

He announces in the same poem, "I know I am deathless," though deathlessness is but vaguely defined. At times, particularly in his later years, he expresses a common and conventional feeling about death and immortality, as in this poem of 1881:

> As at thy portals also death,
> Entering thy sovereign, dim, illimitable grounds,
> To memories of my mother, to the divine blending,
>   maternity,
> To her, buried and gone, yet buried not, gone
>   not from me,
> (I see again the calm benignant face fresh and
>   beautiful still,
> I sit by the form in the coffin,
> I kiss and kiss convulsively again the sweet old
>   lips, the cheeks, the closed eyes in the
>   coffin;)
> To her, the ideal woman, practical, spiritual,
>   of all earth, life, love, to me the best,
> I grave the monumental line before I go, amid
>   these songs,
> And set a tombstone here.

This is scarcely distinguished verse and except that it lacks specific Christian references, is commonplace consolation.

More characteristically, however, death in Whitman is no mere biological fact, but rather a sort of rite of passage, a mystically foreshadowed and necessary way of reunion with cosmic energy—with, if you like, the divine energy. The human spirit, he wrote in 1860,

> ebbs like the ocean, but the cosmic process
> seems forever the same.

The general drift of this attempt to put death into a proper place
in the total scheme of things is to make it part of a Hegelian
triadic resolution, a necessary element in the forever going on-
ward of the world. Life, the thesis, exists, we know not how, and
necessarily produces its antithesis, which is death. But life and
death are in turn subsumed under, or fused into, a universal syn-
thesis that Whitman thinks of sometimes as personal immortality and sometimes as reabsorption into an affirmative cosmic
process that is occasionally identified with God and on other
occasions seems to produce a succession of gods. Whitman's
view is a polar opposite of that of Schopenhauer, in whose
philosophy the ground of all being is a blind cosmic will; Whitman turns this upside down and assumes that the cosmic will is
not blind but purposeful. If one waives any attempt at theological niceties, one can say, I think, that Whitman rests, apparently satisfied, upon something I shall have to call universality.

As with Emerson, so with Whitman: we can in this life be
aware of universality in at least two ways. One is simple observation: we watch the process of things, the pattern of life, the
appearance and disappearance of all phenomena and are forced
to the inference that this ascending pattern must somehow be
sustained by a central dynamic principle. Hence it is that Whitman found no difficulty in weaving evolutionary theory into his
view of the world. But awareness also comes, and this is the
second way, in moments of ecstasy that can occasionally be in-
duced by an intense identification with objects and other persons but that more commonly comes without our bidding. Both
in "Song of Myself" and in "Passage to India" Whitman gives
us notable statements of this supernal sensitivity:

Swiftly arose and spread around me the peace
  and knowledge that pass all the arguments
  of the earth,
And I know that the hand of God is the promise
  of my own,
And I know that the spirit of God is the brother
  of my own,
And that all the men ever born are also my
  brothers, and the women my sisters and
  lovers,
And that a kelson of the creation is love,
And limitless are leaves stiff or drooping
  in the fields,
And brown ants in the little wells beneath
  them,
And messy scabs of the worm fence, heap'd
  stones, elder, mullein and poke-weed.

If one asks why a passage that begins with a line about divine peace and knowledge ends with a line about a worm fence, mullein, and poke-weed, the answer is simply that Whitman at this moment is seeing all phenomena *sub specie aeternitatis*. A poem like "The Mystic Trumpeter" of 1872 is a more extended statement of a like theme; and "Passage to India" concludes with a call to take passage for more than India:

Passage to more than India!
Are thy wings plumed indeed for such far flights?

.   .   .   .

Sail forth—steer for the deep waters only,
Reckless O soul, exploring, I with thee, and
  thou with me,
For we are bound where mariner has not yet
  dared to go,
And we will risk the ship, ourselves and all.

O my brave soul!
O farther, farther sail!

> O daring joy, but safe! are they not all
>   the seas of God?
> O farther, farther, farther sail!

Mystical identification also occurs in Whitman during some warm summer night, or while bathing in the sea, or in a moment of sexual rapture. It is, however, never the product of alcohol, drugs, or any formal religious concentration. If the dear love of comrades, one of Whitman's famous phrases, could be sustained at a sufficiently high level, this might also nourish mystical identification.

It seems probable that only a Christian culture could have produced *Leaves of Grass*. Yet the poem is almost totally without conventional theological terminology. God is an emotional, not a logical, concept, and Whitman does not even attempt definition:

> And I say to mankind, Be not curious about God,
> For I who am curious about each am not curious
>   about God,
> (No array of terms can say how much I am at
>   peace about God and about death.)
> I hear and behold God in every object, yet un-
>   derstand God not in the least,
> Nor do I understand who there can be more
>   wonderful than myself
>
> . . . .
>
> In the faces of men and women I see God and
>   in my own face in the glass,
> I find letters from God dropt in the street,
>   and every one is sign'd by God's name,
> And I leave them where they are, for I know
>   that wheresoe'er I go,
> Others will punctually come for ever and ever.

In the same poem that has this passage ("Song of Myself") there is a lengthy list of deities with which the poet identifies himself, but though the name of Jesus appears elsewhere in Whitman, it is omitted from this catalogue.

Since Whitman will not admit that evil is other than a strand in the great web of being, the concept of inherited sin—indeed, the concept of sin itself—for him has no theological meaning. Salvation likewise is without cosmic sense. In a poem called "This Compost" he is momentarily terrified at the earth, that receptacle for corpses, but he reflects that out of corruption it perpetually brings forth sweetness, so that the Pauline doctrine of the corruptible body and the incorruptible soul also becomes irrelevant. Since every material reality has its spiritual counterpart (Whitman calls it an eidólon), we are as much living in cosmic consciousness now as if we were sent on to heaven in the last promotion of the blest.

As a mystic, Whitman lacks the humility of Oriental systems of belief. He stands imperturbable in the midst of nature. If God, whatever Whitman means by God, is great and proud, Whitman, his replica, is justified in being great and proud also. Order in man's spiritual essence parallels order in that vitalism which is the essence of the universe. And so Whitman could write in a short poem of 1860, entitled "Kosmos," this general statement of personal identification with all imaginable states of being anywhere at any time:

> Who includes diversity and is Nature,
> Who is the amplitude of the earth, and the
>   coarseness and sexuality of the earth,
>   and the great charity of the earth,
>   and the equilibrium also,
> Who has not look'd forth from the windows of
>   the eyes for nothing, or whose brain
>   held audience with messengers for
>   nothing,

Who contain believers and disbelievers,
    who is the most majestic lover,
Who holds duly his or her triune proportion
    of realism, spiritualism, and of the
    aesthetic or intellectual,
Who having consider'd the body finds all its
    organs and parts good,
Who, out of the theory of the earth and of
    his or her body understands by subtle
    analogies all other theories,
The theory of a city, a poem, and of the large
    politics of these States;
Who believes not only in our globe with its
    sun and moon, but in other globes with
    their suns and moons,
Who, constructing the house of himself or
    herself, not for a day but for all time,
    sees races, eras, dates, generations,
The past, the future, dwelling there, like
    space, inseparable together.

Possibly the syntax of this poem is a little to seek; but it seems to express forcefully and in small compass the central belief of Whitman in a divine principle of universal vitalism that, by reason of its emphasis upon activism rather than passivity, is curiously American.

⟶ V ⟵

THE PESSIMISM OF MARK TWAIN

I

Bᴇʀɴᴀʀᴅ DᴇVᴏᴛᴏ somewhere remarks that you can quote Mark Twain on almost any side of any question, and the student soon discovers this is true. Thus Twain wrote an essay excoriating King Leopold's cruelty in the Congo and another one denouncing Western imperialism; yet, after going around the world, when he published *Following the Equator*, he was full of praise for the British empire because it had imposed cleanliness, order, and a sense for progress upon the countries the British occupied. In a book on Christian Science he denounced Mrs. Eddy as essentially fraudulent as a prophet and essentially crafty as a businesswoman; but he told his official biographer, Albert Bigelow Paine, that Mrs. Eddy likely deserved a place in the Trinity as much as the other members of it because she had organized a healing principle that had been employed for two thousand years as mere guesswork. No one was more vituperative than he about the covetousness of the robber barons, and the novel by Twain and Warner, *The Gilded Age*, gave its name to that period. Twain, however, sought to make money by seeking out and owning monopolies as they did, he had golden visions of easy wealth, and in his lawless egotism he resembled the millionaires whom he denounced. He had no use for kings, so that *A Connecticut Yankee in King Arthur's Court* was written among other purposes to ridicule monarchy; but Twain gloried in the attention paid him by William II of Germany, the Prince of Wales, and the Austrian royal family. Indeed, his essay on the assassination of the Austrian empress soon leaves this theme for a dazzle of rhetorical delight in the pomp of a military funeral illustrating the might of imperial power. Twain delighted to ridicule bathos; he thought, however, that his sentimental *The Prince and the Pauper* was a better work of art than *The Adventures of Tom Sawyer*, and regarded the equally sentimental *Personal Recollections of Joan of Arc* as his literary masterpiece. These conflicts were, apparently, built into him. The genial humorist of William Dean Howells' *My Mark Twain*, printed in 1910, is one side of him, and the tortured personality of Justin Kaplan's magisterial *Mr. Clemens and Mark Twain*, published in 1966, is another.

Such complexities have to be sorted out, and there is an inevitable tendency to arrange the components of Twain's personality in pairs, or, as Emerson would say, polarities. During most of the humorist's life the polarities were between the picture of Twain as a popular funny man, and the emerging assumption that he was a literary genius. Another set of contradictory interpretations is represented by two notable early studies: Van Wyck Brooks's *The Ordeal of Mark Twain*, which argued in 1920 that a naïve Western genius was made to submit to the genteel tradition as represented by Mrs. Clemens and Twain's literary friend, Howells; and DeVoto's *Mark Twain's America*, which maintained in 1932 that Brooks knew nothing about either Missouri or the West and that Twain was from the beginning a conscious Western literary artist. I suppose a third rearrangement is implicit in the subtitle of De Lancey Ferguson's excellent biography of 1943, *Mark Twain: Man and Legend*. By the forties the public personality of Clemens had developed into legend, but there was now far more material at hand to use for painting the actual man.

When one asks what Twain really believed about God, man, and the universe, is there any way to fuse these opposites into a single pair? I think there is. The contradictions that make Twain interesting from this point of view seem to me to arise from the fact that from an early period there was in him an acceptance, perhaps naïve, of eighteenth-century rationalism, which easily absorbed into itself doctrines of comparative religion and of evolution dominant in the nineteenth century. But there was also from boyhood an opposite tendency, a kind of romantic sensibility which looks like nineteenth-century subjectivism and in one sense is that, but which really descends from eighteenth-century sentimentalism in both the popular and the philosophic sense. In Twain the spirits of Voltaire and Rousseau fought for control. In him the deism of Tom Paine and the materialism of somebody like Haeckel struggled with a stubborn temperamental conviction that individual goodness counts—a belief all his naïve determinism could never extinguish. Twain denounced all organized religion, and, in his privately printed "gospel" of 1906, *What Is Man?* he stripped the human being of free will and destroyed the possibility of self-determined personal development. Yet Twain's best friend, aside from Howells, was the Rev. Joseph Twichell of Hartford; and Twain always had a weakness for clergymen unless, like the Rev. Mr. Sabine, who refused to bury an actor from his New York church, they seemed to him sanctimonious. He told Paine in 1903, "Who can doubt that society in heaven consists of mainly undesirable persons?" But when Twain's wife died in 1904, he had this inscription engraved on her tombstone: "Gott sei dir gnädig, O meine Wonne!" It is difficult to see how God could be gracious to Olivia Clemens in the afterlife unless there was some heaven for her to go to. Yet Twain had earlier declared that if God had prepared such a place for us and really wanted us to know about it, He could have found some better medium of communication than the Bible, a book "so liable to alterations and misinterpretation." The point is not to trap the great humorist—it is absurdly easy to do so; the point is to try to comprehend the major phases of his erratic development in the matter of belief.

II

It is commonly held that the determinism of *What Is Man?* and the general pessimism of Twain's utterance about the human race are products of the Calvinism that was drilled into him in boyhood. Calvinism is, however, an intricate system of ideas that has many variants, and I think those who really accepted Calvinism and later broke with it all had to go through a period of spiritual agony. I do not find any such period in Twain's biography—anything resembling that chronicled in, for example, William Hale White's *The Autobiography of Mark Rutherford*, which is only partly fiction, or in Edmund Gosse's *Father and Son*, which is wholly fact. The simple village preaching and the simple village teaching to which young Samuel Clemens was exposed contained nothing, so far as I can see, like "Sinners in the Hands of an Angry God," however revivalism may have described damnation. Religion in Hannibal seems to have been the standard religion of the Bible belt. It is true that in both *Tom Sawyer* and *Huck Finn* Twain plays up the boys' fear of damnation, fear of the devil, and fear of instant judgment if they do something wrong. He also plays up their fear of witchcraft. Are we therefore to argue that witchcraft was generally taught in the churches? Most of our information about Sam Clemens' boyhood and his boyhood religion comes from Sam Clemens, the adult writer, so that it is difficult to know how much is true and how much is imagined in his recollections. Young Sam detested Sunday school and church-going as most boys do; like any other boy he was afraid of God and juvenile about the meaning of prayer. He also picked up a good deal of folklore from the Negroes and from his playmates. But I am unable to see much dour Calvinism in this experience. If he had been taught any kind of Calvinism, and if this had been really ground into him, we should have heard later how he struggled with the concepts of damnation, election, and efficacious grace through Jesus Christ, but, except for the chapters on Palestine in *Innocents Abroad*, where Twain could not avoid the topic, the name of Jesus scarcely appears in his work. He concentrates on God—on the concept of a Christian God, which Twain thinks of as a human invention designed to flatter mankind into the belief that man is of any consequence in the universe.

From 1853, when he left home, until 1870, when he married Olivia Langdon, Samuel Clemens was a wanderer on the face of the earth—a wandering printer, a wandering newspaperman, a wandering writer, a Mississippi River pilot traveling up and down some 1400 miles of shifting channel, an amateur miner, a popular lecturer of the comic kind, and on occasions virtually a vagabond. Much of this period was spent on the frontier; for instance, Nevada, or in territory that had recently been frontier territory; for example, the great river. There were cities, towns, hamlets, and plantations along the Mississippi exhibiting considerable culture, but the restless population of the stream itself was made up of raftsmen, keelboatmen, gamblers, fancy women, slave-traders with their coffles of human merchandise, roustabouts, profane mates, itinerant evangelists, medicine men, and other like human types, most of them rakish, few of them having any permanent place in stable society. A journeyman printer, moreover, sees more of the seamy side of life than he does of its gentler aspects. A newspaperman is usually better acquainted with sinfulness than he is with salvation. Nevada, when Twain went there, was a boom-and-bust frontier area, and so were the parts of California he knew. The Hawaiian Islands were less crude, but at this time they were in a state I can describe only as a quiet and comfortable anarchy.

As a lecturer after 1866 Twain knew more about hotels than he did about homes; and when he joined the *Quaker City* excursion to the Mediterranean in 1867, he was still the rover, still the wild humorist of the Pacific slope, still the restless younger man conscious of talent but ignorant of the proper channel through which to direct its flow. Twain did not achieve anything resembling stability until he was about forty. For twenty years his experience had been of the capriciousness of luck, the meaninglessness of mere good will, the crass cruelty of chance, as when the steamboat *Pennsylvania* blew up and killed 150 persons, including his brother, the amiable Henry Clemens. The God who seemed to preside over the anarchy that ruled the world from the Mississippi to the Hawaiian Islands was no genteel Christian deity, but the indifferent God of Thomas Hardy. Twain's twenty years of wandering were, I suggest, far more influential in molding his outlook than the mild Christianity of Hannibal, Missouri, which in later years seemed to him an utterly inadequate explanation of the ways of God to man.

I believe one can distinguish three shaping elements in these decades. The first is that during these years, Clemens read enormously at every opportunity and that much of his reading had an eighteenth-century basis or bias, whether it was *Songs in Many Keys* by that most Augustan of Boston poets, Oliver Wendell Holmes, virtually memorized by Twain when he was ill in Hawaii, or the three great memoir writers whom he read and reread—Saint-Simon, Pepys, and Casanova. He seems to have used Voltaire as a means for learning French. Above all, while he was a pilot, he saturated himself in Paine's *The Age of Reason*, so that when, on the *Quaker City* excursion, he read the Bible with some care as a guide to Palestine, he approached religious doctrine with a deistic bias. One should add that he was fascinated by science, particularly astronomy and geology, and could conceive of no other universe than the Newtonian one.

A second episode of basic importance was Twain's meeting with an enigmatic Scotsman named MacFarlane in Cincinnati in 1856–57. It is possible that MacFarlane never existed. If he did, he lived by himself, he was a serious-minded worker, and he had read widely in contemporary science and philosophy. He believed in evolution, regarding man as a failure, the only animal capable of malice and uncleanliness. If Twain is to be trusted, MacFarlane apparently laid the foundation for the humorist's future conviction that the moral sense in man is what degrades him below the animals.

The third impact of these years, particularly those on the Mississippi and covering his experiences in the Far West, was brooding over vastness—the vastness of nights on the river when, alone in the pilot-house, he had to travel through darkness, the vastness of the starry heavens, the immense indifference of sky and land in the Nevada desert and of sky and sea in the Pacific, where most of the crew of the *Hornet* had miserably perished.

He adopted the Newtonian view that the universe is an immense machine created and supervised by an infinitely remote engineer. He adopted also from his readings in popular astronomy concepts of the enormity of space and the littleness of the solar system. Seeing then and later the perpetual imbecility of the human race, having small opportunity and no desire to attend church services, he arrived early at the conclusion that Christian altruism, Christian salvation, Christian benevolence were incompetent measures of the majestic indifference of God, the mercilessness of the heavens, and the unbreakable chain that bound one event to its successor. These views he long suppressed or put aside, though they lurk in much that he wrote from *Innocents Abroad* to *Pudd'nhead Wilson*, and though they appear, imaginatively powerful or logically expressed, in such works as *The Man That Corrupted Hadleyburg*, *The $30,000 Bequest*, and *Was It Heaven or Hell?* and, more powerfully still, in posthumous works like *The Mysterious Stranger* and *Letters from the Earth*. Of course there is also *What Is Man?*, a book that gets its title from the Psalms: "What is man, that thou regardest him, or the son of man, that thou visitest him?" Twain's answer is: "Not much."

Remembering that Mark Twain perpetually contradicts himself, I think we can yet sketch out the lines of his mature interpretation of God, man, and the universe. God is a being of majestical and unpredictable power, who in Twain's fiction retains most of the characteristics of the Christian deity as a *dramatis persona* except benevolence toward man, but whose essence Twain never clearly defines. God is, however, the ground of being of the universe, which, at some remote point in time He created by arbitrary fiat—or perhaps the fiat was not arbitrary, a point to which I shall come in a moment. What Twain means by the universe is not always clear. Mostly it is a universe of matter that works, or is worked upon, by mechanical principles. Yet, as Young Satan informs the boys in *The Mysterious Stranger*, the universe is a dream, they are dreams and God Himself is a dream. The point would be unimportant except that, after the manner of Newton and his commentators, Twain makes his deity give matter an initial push, a first action, and from this first act every other event mercilessly follows. Whether the law of cause and effect existed intellectually prior to the universe, so that the operation of matter had to conform to that law, Twain does not say, nor does he define deity in any clear and consistent terms. Does God conform to necessity, or is necessity something imposed upon the universe by God? In the splendid rhetorical opening of *Letters from the Earth* Mark Twain pictures creation after the manner of Milton and has the archangels comment on it, as do the archangels in Goethe's *Faust*. The attributes of Twain's deity, like his acts, are phrased in Christian terms, but his God is not a Christian God.

Although Mark Twain insists in *What Is Man?* and elsewhere—for example, in *Pudd'nhead Wilson*—upon mechanical necessity, the mechanical universe is somehow also an evolutionary universe, somewhat to the confusion of Twain's metaphor about man as a machine—a metaphor that carries one back to La Mettrie and other eighteenth-century French *philosophes*. As a machine, man has no control over his acts or his motives for action. He is merely an impersonal engine, moved, directed, and commanded, says Twain, by external influences only. He cannot think an original thought nor perform a uniquely self-willed action. Behind the elaborate façade of religious and ethical systems there is, says Twain, the basic truth that the only motive for action is self-approval. How a machine arrives at self-approval Twain does not quite explain. Yet man the machine can also, apparently of its own volition, place itself in circumstances that will, as this writer says, "train it" in an upward or downward direction, morally and socially. How a machine determines what is subjectively upward or down, again, is not made plain, and Twain seems content with a virtually insoluble paradox: Man is an impersonal engine commanded by external influences only, but this impersonal engine is also subjectively conscious of the need of nourishing its own self-approval.

This self-approval—and here, I take it, is Twain's attempt to get out of the difficulty—seems to be a function of conscience, which Twain describes as "that mysterious autocrat, lodged in a man, which compels the man to content its desires." Twain is again fuzzy. If conscience is something like Schopenhauer's irrational will, it is not conscience but something unconscious and instinctual; and if conscience is, as Twain says it is, indifferent to "man's greed," indifference to good fails to throw any light upon the origin of "good" as a way by which to measure the consciousness of being conscious of good. At times conscience seems to be a synonym for the Moral Sense, Twain's favorite whipping boy; but the moral sense, or at least a sense for the higher good, undergoes an odd transformation when the Old Man in the dialog tells the Young Man; "Diligently train your ideals upward and still upward toward a summit where you will find your chief pleasure in conduct which, while contenting you, will be sure to confer benefits upon your neighbor." This is a queer parallel to Adam Smith's theory that although all men regard their own individual interests only, each is led as by an invisible hand to work for the good of the whole; and the difficulty is not met by saying that idealism is simply another form of self-regard; the difficulty is to explain how any concept of public good can possibly arise.

What Is Man? purports to be a systematic treatise, but its logical difficulties are so patent as to require little further discussion. Obviously Twain changes the concept of a machine to suit his argument. A machine is in fact a mechanical object lacking all consciousness and unable to perform the function for which it was built unless suitable outside force is intelligently applied to set it in motion. For Twain to talk about a machine of steel as being more "civilized" than a machine of stone is a case of a transferred epithet that conceals a logical error. Machines are not civilized; they are produced by civilization. Machines have no consciousness; man does. A machine cannot either by volition or instinct reproduce its kind. This is possible only to organisms, which, though they may have statistically predictable potentialities, are more than, or at least other than, mere elementary matter. No machine can train itself even in Twain's sense of moving, physically or psychologically, into some sort of social and temporal area where "outside influences"—his phrase —will somehow improve the machine morally, intellectually, or socially. Machines can be improved mechanically but not otherwise. In truth Twain never distinguished between a mechanical concept like that of a machine and a biological concept like that of an organism.

His basic assumption is of course that of much modern science until the twentieth century: the iron necessity in cause and effect as the "explanation" of events. It was axiomatic and primary in most of the books about science that he read. If one wanted to take Twain's assumption seriously, one would have to point out that in our time Heisenberg's uncertainty principle damages this primary postulate beyond repair. The principles of the new physics, as Arthur H. Compton has said, cannot predict any event; they can tell only the chance of its occurrence. Even the behavior of an organism is not something that can be definitely determined; the utmost one can say is that its behavior will fall within certain principles or limits of probability. But statistics of chance are one thing; necessity is another. The curious thing is that Twain, despite his argument, was imaginatively enlisted on the side of chance. Thus in *The Mysterious Stranger* Young Satan, who possesses supernal power, at the request of the boys of Eseldorf actively interferes to change the already determined patterns of the lives of some of the villagers. How, if the iron law of necessity rules the universe, can even an archangel alter the course of events, especially in view of the fact that Twain says elsewhere, "Even the Almighty Himself cannot check or change [the] sequence of events once it is started"? Is an angel somehow more powerful than the Almighty?

III

It is of course possible, as DeVoto remarks, that the gospel of *What Is Man?* is not really a serious statement of determinism but rather a plea for pardon. If man is helpless, man cannot be blamed for anything. This is emotionally possible; yet the logical difficulty arises: who is to do the pardoning? And at this point some suspicion of a Calvinist influence truly arises, since, if God determines all, God is the only competent pardoning power. On the other hand, if the iron law of necessity existed anterior to the fiat of God, not even God is competent to forgive, unless, indeed, we blur all distinctions and declare that everything is as it is because it is as it is—a generalization that gets us precisely nowhere for it strips all words of all general meanings.

However this may be, we are dealing with a great imaginative writer, not with a metaphysician; and when we turn to Twain's concept of what he often referred to as the damned human race, we find a continuing tension between the ideas of Voltaire and the ideas of Rousseau; or, more particularly, we find that Twain in his maturer years takes over the notion of Swift, who said he hated and detested that animal called man, although he heartily loved John, Peter, Thomas, and so forth.

We may begin with some characteristic expressions of the darker view of man by Twain. The heir of all the ages in the foremost files of time seemed to our writer mostly a failure. He wrote somewhere that man was made at the end of the week's work when God was tired. He told Albert Bigelow Paine that man

is a rickety sort of a thing, anyway you take him, a regular British Museum of infirmities and inferiorities. He is always undergoing repairs. . . . man starts as a child and lives on diseases to the end as a regular diet. . . . [Man is] the animal of the wig, the ear-trumpet, the glass eye, the porcelain teeth, the wooden leg, the trepanned skull, the silver wind-pipe—a creature that is mended and patched all over from top to bottom.

I quote only a part of this diatribe, which, however, ends by claiming for man one tremendous superiority over the other animals—in his imagination, his intellect. Yet on another occasion Twain informed Paine that anybody who knew anything knew that there was not a single life that was ever lived that was worth living.

The assumption that man's imagination marks his superiority appears many times in Twain, but this tribute is countered by the argument that in being gifted with a moral sense, man was given opportunity to degrade himself below the animals, and used it. This being true, only the mad can be happy. Satan in *The Mysterious Stranger* demonstrates to the boys that man's cruelty to man is always the product of the moral sense, but Twain's most straightforward statement about this degrading quality appears in a document posthumously published in *Letters from the Earth*, entitled "The Lowest Animal." Here are some statements from it:

> One is obliged to concede that in true loftiness of character, Man cannot claim to approach even the meanest of the Higher Animals. It is plain that he is constitutionally incapable of approaching that altitude; that he is constitutionally afflicted with a Defect which must make such approach forever impossible, for it is manifest that this defect is permanent in him, indestructible, ineradicable.
>
> I find this Defect to be the *Moral Sense*. He is the only animal that has it. It is the secret of degradation. It is the quality *which enables him to do wrong*. It has no other office. It is incapable of performing any other function. It could never have been intended to perform any other. Without it, man could do no wrong. He would rise at once to the level of the Higher Animals.
>
> It is as valueless to him as is disease. . . . What . . . do we find the Primal Curse to have been? Plainly what it was in the beginning: the infliction upon man of the Moral Sense; the ability to distinguish good from evil; and with it, necessarily, the ability to *do* evil; for there can be no evil act without the presence of consciousness of it in the doer of it.[1]

The emotional tone of such passages is Swiftian, but the irony, though savage, has, as it were, a Voltairean base, since the concept of a moral sense or moral faculty was commonplace in eighteenth-century philosophy, and the reasoning behind Twain's satire is reasoning that derives its picture of man's imperfection by the use of Right Reason. I am of course using the term "eighteenth century" loosely and not chronologically.

Twain got himself into another logical difficulty. He holds, as we have seen, that man is a machine with no will of its own,

[1] Bernard DeVoto, ed., *Mark Twain, Letters from the Earth* (New York, 1962), pp. 228–29. The statement about man as a museum of infirmities is repeated in this essay.

that everything which happens is predetermined by an unbreakable chain of cause and effect beginning with some primordial
act, that man is without free will, and that any progress which
appears in humanity is solely the result of being somehow exposed to a better environment or conditioning. But this machine
is also endowed with consciousness, and in *What Is Man?*
Twain also gives it a conscience, although conscience is here not
a function of free will but a mysterious autocrat lodged in man
and compelling him to content its desires, which are apparently
to be distinguished from the desires of the man who has the
conscience. Conscience is likewise declared to be indifferent to
the good of man, though what is meant by "good" does not
clearly appear.

How does the moral sense fit into the machine? In all Twain's
discussions of the moral sense he seems to assume that the moral
sense enables man to know the good, yet, knowing the good,
man invariably chooses evil. This choice must therefore be vol-
untary. We must then also assume either that the moral sense is
part of the automatic functioning of man the machine, in which
case praise and blame like good and evil are totally irrelevant; or
that the moral sense, whether thought of as a faculty of the
mind other than conscience or as some phase or function of
consciousness, freely chooses to make value judgments, which
man's willfulness invariably ignores and, in fact, uses as guides to
proceed in the direction of evil rather than of good. I say that
the moral sense must be a faculty of the mind other than conscience simply because Twain has elsewhere defined conscience
as an autocrat which is other than free will and does not seek the
good of man.

Whatever the confusion of Twain's logic, man is for him,
patently, a hypocritical being. Like all satirists but more savage-

ly than any other American satirist except Ambrose Bierce, he delights to dwell upon the discrepancy in the moral world between appearance and reality. He makes this point over and over again. Thus Huck Finn always sees through sanctimoniousness. Thus Twain not once but many times satirizes Sunday-school morality and its accompanying moral tales. Such an exposure is a governing theme in *The Gilded Age, Pudd'nhead Wilson,* and *A Connecticut Yankee,* in short stories like *The Man That Corrupted Hadleyburg* and in many of the essays, as in the instance of Twain's defense of Harriet Shelley, which was published in the writer's lifetime, and "The War Prayer," which was not. Twain has an enormous contempt for the biblical God and for the Bible, both of which he regards as man's invention, an equally enormous contempt for modern Christian governments, a good-natured contempt for most churches and most religions, and a sardonic delight in showing up the difference between official theories of ethics, usually Christian, and the actual motives and conduct of men.

IV

But Twain was also, whether he knew it or not, an eighteenth-century sentimentalist; that is, he really believed that any example of goodness could touch the feeling heart and make men instantly better. Most of the psychological changes in his stories have the instant quality of Christian conversion. If Twain lacked Rousseau's faith in natural man, he certainly seems to have preferred men in natural environments to men in courts and cities. He looked back with nostalgia upon his life in Missouri, his experience on the Mississippi, his years as a miner, his trip to Lake Tahoe with one companion. Huck Finn and Nigger Jim are two of nature's noblemen as the American claimant in the novel of that name is not—he is merely one of nature's fools. Our author is indulgent toward Colonel Sellers with all his folly, product as that character is of a village culture, but he is merciless upon King Leopold, product of a sophisticated court. True, Twain was also attracted by persons having and exercising power —Henry Rogers, the Standard Oil millionaire, Slade, the murderer in charge of the Overland Express, General Grant, whose moral deficiencies Twain totally neglects. But more important is it to realize that for Twain some human beings totally escape the inglorious human predicament. Such a one was Joan of Arc. Such another was Olivia Clemens. In fact it would be easy to go through his writings and cull out instance after instance of human generosity, saintliness, self-sacrifice, and humility that totally contradict his officially cynical attitude toward altruism. These cases he would be logically forced to categorize as instances of self-deceit, but I find no indication he takes this approach in recording the lives of those he loved and admired. He stood up for the Negro, the Jew, and the Chinaman. One of his favorite adjectives is "noble," and if he often uses it satirically, he also employs it with entire seriousness to characterize a great man or a great action.

Indeed, it is possible to turn my entire analysis upside down— to say that in condemning the Christian God, the Bible, Christian history, the churches, and the Christian world, irascible, passionate, short-tempered, and egotistical as he frequently was, Twain was the foremost Christian of them all. He judged Christianity not by its performance but by its principle. He appealed from Christian fact to Christian idealism. Like Emerson he thought the best thing a Christian could do was to abandon Christianity altogether. Twain's indictment of cruelty, past, present, and to come, is an indictment possible only to a man who truly believes he should love his neighbor, fear God, and keep His commandments. What Twain asked the world was that it permit Christianity to sit in judgment upon Christianity. How else explain at once his gentleness to most children and all animals, his patience with his invalid wife and his unpredictable brother Orion, and his hatred of hypocrisy, his rages against injustice, inhumanity, and war? If he thought the human race ought to be damned or perhaps was already damned, it is still true that damnation is a Christian concept; and it can be argued with great plausibility that Twain's remote cosmic God is no more than an expansion of the God of Job:

> Canst thou bind the chains of the Pleiades,
>   Or loose the bands of Orion?
> Canst thou lead forth the Mazzaroth in their season?
>   Or canst thou guide the Bear with her sons?
>
> . . . .
>
> Who then is able to stand before Me?
> Who hath given Me anything beforehand,
>   that I should repay him?

One of the most poignant incidents in all Mark Twain is to be found in *Captain Stormfield's Visit to Heaven*, originally intended as a burlesque on Elizabeth Stuart Phelps's *Gates Ajar*. On his way through space to heaven Captain Stormfield has gone off course to race with a comet, and fetches up at the wrong gate. There he is asked to identify his place of origin. He tries San Francisco, then California, then the United States of America, then the New World, all in vain. He then says he comes from the world, and the angel who is serving as a clerk brusquely replies that there are billions of them. Somewhat humbled, the captain by and by returns and pleads: "I don't seem to make out which world it is I'm from. But you may know it from this—it's the one the Saviour saved." The clerk bends his head gently at the Name, and responds: "The worlds He has saved are like to the gates of heaven in number—no one can count them." Tom Paine, whom Mark Twain often resembles, could not have written this scene. But Paine might have written another sentence by Mark Twain: "To trust the God of the Bible is to trust an irascible, vindictive, fierce and ever fickle and changeful master.'"

What, then, did Mark Twain think? At some time in the 1880's, if the Paine biography is to be believed, he set down a formal creed in nine successive paragraphs; and though he later departed from many of the several articles, within limits the text gives us the general declaration of faith from which, despite his growing pessimism, Twain did not essentially depart. It begins by stating his belief in the existence of God. It goes on to say that he does not believe God ever sent a message to man by anybody and that He never made himself visible to mortal eyes. Twain thinks the Old and New Testaments were imagined and written by men. Since—and here Twain *is* in line with Tom Paine and Franklin—the goodness, justice, and mercy of God are manifested in His works, Twain thinks they are also manifested to man here now and hereafter. He does not believe in special providences or miracles. He cannot see any value in eternal punishment. He is indifferent about personal immortality. He thinks the moral principles of the world are the outcome of the experience of the world. And he concludes with this striking statement:

If I break these moral laws I cannot see how I injure God by it, for He is beyond the reach of injury from me—I could as easily injure a planet by throwing mud at it. It seems to me that my misconduct could only injure me and other men. I cannot benefit God by obeying these moral laws—I could as easily benefit the planet by withholding my mud. . . . Consequently I do not see why I should be either punished or rewarded hereafter for the deeds I do here.

If Twain had stuck to this, he would have merely revived the tradition of deism. But with increasing pessimism, the affirmative teleology of the eighteenth century was no longer possible, not merely because of Twain's personal disappointments, but also because developments in science and philosophy made it increasingly difficult to maintain that the earth was made for man.

Twain's pessimism did more than mirror his personal bitterness. It partook of the quality of an important current in late nineteenth-century speculative thought. As Herbert Schneider has said, idealism and agnosticism have been constants in American philosophy; and despite Josiah Royce, despite the Social Gospel, despite populism in politics and the idealism of thinkers like Howison and societies like the Ethical Culture group, the traditional doctrine of inevitable progress in a free democratic society was, in the view of many, overshadowed in the last quarter of that century by despair. The after-effects of the Gilded Age included a growing skepticism about the inevitability of the American dream. The panics of 1873 and 1893 shook men's confidence in business progress, nor were the alternatives presented by anarchism and communism attractive. The American reception of Darwin's *The Descent of Man*, published in 1871, was mixed; but all parties to the controversy it aroused were compelled to admit, explicitly or implicitly, that man was now vastly lower than the angels. Social Darwinism emphasized competitiveness; and though one could argue that evolution meant an inevitable progress in society and perhaps improvement in individuals, the argument was equally plausible that neither church nor state could alter the world of nature red in tooth and claw. A rugged thinker like William Graham Sumner reduced moral energy to the energy of competing individuals, and in that free-for-all battle the forgotten man was the *petit bourgeois*, the man of good will, the average middle-class American as the average American pictured himself and his world. The assumption that in a closed universe energy dissipates and that modern civilization hastens this dissipation drove both Henry Adams and Brooks Adams into cosmic despair. For them modern life was a struggle between fear and greed in a nightmare out of which, at least for Henry Adams, the only escape was a modern mystique about the medieval Virgin, whom he opposed to the dynamo, which concentrated and exhausted force. In the Harvard yard a group of young poets, among them Edwin Arlington Robinson, George Santayana, and Trumbull Stickney, took refuge in either Schopenhauerian despair, an austere stoicism, or a kind of desperate Epicurean outlook. The vogue in this country of Fitz-Gerald's version of the *Rubáiyát* of Omar Khayyám was enormous; whole clubs were formed to read it and in a modest way carry out its principle of eat, drink, and be merry, for tomorrow we die. A bitter novel like E. L. Voynich's *The Gadfly*, a tour de force published in 1897, swept through intellectual circles, and by and by was to sell its hundreds of thousands of copies in Russia because it was supposed to represent the death of God. Indeed, it was against the widespread *fin de siècle* spirit that Theodore Roosevelt preached his naïve gospel of physical activity for the sake of physical activity. The mood of the period, or at least this aspect of it, was well expressed by William Vaughn Moody in his poem, "Gloucester Moors," two stanzas of which I shall cite. He compares the earth to a ship and queries:

> God, dear God! Does she know her port,
> Though she goes so far about?
> Or blind astray, does she make her sport
> To brazen and chance it out?
> I watched when her captains passed:

She were better captainless.
Men in the cabin, before the mast,
But some were reckless and some aghast,
And some sat gorged at mess.

. . . .

. . . thou, vast outbound ship of souls,
What harbor town for thee?
What shapes, when thy arriving tolls,
Shall crowd the banks to see?
Shall all the happy shipmates then
Stand singing brotherly?
Or shall a haggard ruthless few
Warp her over and bring her to,
While the many broken souls of men
Fester down in the slaver's pen,
And nothing to say or do?

To this skepticism, this nescience, the idealism of Emerson and the optimism of Whitman had apparently come at last, at least for many sensitive souls. It was not Mark Twain but Henry Adams who wrote:

For the first time, the stage-scenery of the senses collapsed; the human mind felt itself stripped naked, vibrating in a void of shapeless energies, with resistless mass, colliding, crushing, wasting, and destroying what these same energies had created and labored from eternity to perfect. Society became fantastic, a vision of pantomime with a mechanical motion; and its so-called thought merged in the mere sense of life, and pleasure in the sense. . . . God might be, as the Church said, a Substance, but He could not be a Person.

In the matter of cosmic pessimism Mark Twain was not unique; he was in some sense representative of a whole tendency in religion and philosophy.

∗ VI ∗

THE COSMIC LONELINESS OF
ROBERT FROST

I

W E COME NOW to Robert Frost, whom I have chosen as a representative American man of letters for the twentieth century. I do so because, though he was born in 1874, he published nothing of importance until *A Boy's Will* appeared in 1913, one year after the beginning of the poetic renaissance in this country with the founding of *Poetry: A Magazine of Verse* in Chicago. Frost was born in San Francisco; in 1914 *North of Boston* associated him with New England; he became a poet in residence at the University of Michigan in 1921; he later bought property in Florida and sometimes wintered in Texas; and as a lecturer and "sayer" of his poems he traveled over the entire continental United States. If he wrote "The Death of the Hired Man" about upper New England, he wrote "Once by the Pacific" about the California coast. He knew the United States better than Emerson or Whitman did; and nothing is more thoroughly characteristic of this knowledge than a poem in *A Further Range* (1936) called "A Record Stride." The writer contemplates a pair of old shoes in a bedroom closet and says:

I touch my tongue to the shoes now
And unless my sense is at fault,
On one I can taste Atlantic,
On the other Pacific, salt.

The poem hints that Frost has tried to measure the country and get the United States stated. He so far succeeded that he was, I think, the only American poet who had a president of the United States come to assist at the dedication of a library in his honor while the poet was still alive, just as he was the only writer called to participate officially in a presidential inauguration. Others among his contemporaries may spring immediately to mind in this matter of literature and belief—T. S. Eliot for his high Anglicanism, Conrad Aiken for his cosmic mysticism, Robinson Jeffers for his inhumanism—but Frost is more widely read. The Israeli government invited him to that country when they wanted a representative American author, and the State Department sponsored his visit to Russia in 1962.

If his acquaintance with the continental United States was thus extraordinary, we have also to note the enormous revolutions that occurred during the long span of his life. When Frost was born, U. S. Grant was still president of the United States; when he died the first Roman Catholic was in the White House. The poet lived through the panic of 1893, the bitter Bryan-McKinley campaign of 1896, the Spanish-American War, the Russo-Japanese War, both Balkan wars, World War I, the Russian Revolution, the rise of Hitler, World War II, the Korean War, the Bay of Pigs episode, and the beginning of our troubles in Southeast Asia. During his life there were invented the telephone, X-rays, the radio, the motion picture, television, the automobile, the airplane, the Xerox machine, the electric typewriter, the vacuum cleaner, the atom bomb, the nuclear submarine, and

117

a thousand other conveniences and inconveniences, successes and disasters we now take for granted. When Frost was born, Alaska, Arizona, Colorado, Hawaii, Idaho, Montana, New Mexico, North Dakota, Oklahoma, South Dakota, Utah, Washington, and Wyoming had not yet entered the union. In 1874 about three-fourths of the population lived on farms or in villages, and only one-fourth in cities; today these fractions are reversed. It took Frost's widowed mother more than four days and nights to go by train from Oakland, California, to Lawrence, Massachusetts. In 1880, when Frost was six, the population of the country was a little more than 50 million. Today it is over 190 million. Yet this swinger of birches, this poet of the natural as opposed to the metropolitan environment of man, kept the allegiance of hundreds of thousands of readers and listeners, most of whom had never seen rural New England and few of whom felt much need to be versed in country things. I can think of no other American poet who witnessed more social, political, moral, religious, and scientific revolutions. Not unnaturally Frost became not so much a man as an institution. How shall one deal with this legendary, this mythological, being?

Let us begin with the personality and the *persona*, the man and the mask. It is in no way discreditable that the public image of a writer is not necessarily consonant with his private personality. We have seen the discrepancy in Mark Twain between the kindly and quotable public sage with the bushy eyebrows, the humorous drawl, and Samuel L. Clemens in private life, boastful, savagely unkind, remorseful, gentle, sentimental, profane, and often untrustworthy in matters of fact. The same disharmony is in Frost. On the one hand the public image of the country philosopher, the homely popular poet, the sayer of poems so seemingly transparent anybody could understand them; on the other hand the bitter and confused young man of Lawrance Thompson's biography, or so much of it as has appeared—almost a beatnik, without roots or local attachment, irresponsible, moody, vindictive, untruthful, altruistic by fits and starts, vaguely aware that he was in the world for something but unable to find out his true vocation until he was nearing forty. If Frost had died when *A Boy's Will* was published, he would have been catalogued as a minor lyric poet. The fact that *North of Boston* came out when he was forty gives a kind of uniformity to all his later work, as if it were all one big volume. But the fact also conceals the tortured ways by which Frost slowly fought his way to a philosophy and a vocation.

The Thompson biography, various collections of letters, books of reminiscence more or less trustworthy, and various commentaries on Frost permit us to sort out one or two shaping elements during the four dark early decades of the poet's life. One notes the haziness of his religious upbringing. In his letter proposing marriage, the poet's father, William P. Frost, told his mother, Isabelle Moodie: "You are a Christian—I am not." Presumably this discord, together with the father's obvious irresponsibility as a bread-winner, did not make for family stability. The mother was first a Presbyterian, then a Unitarian, and finally a Swedenborgian but, so far as I can make out, a Swedenborgian of sentimental vagueness. The boy was baptized in the Swedenborgian church and was taught the usual Bible stories, and there is also some trace of Kierkegaardian fear and trembling in his mature verse, but I cannot find that he was subjected to any thorough theological discipline, albeit his mother told him tales of great heroes who died for the faith that was in them, wrote fairy stories, and compensated for her unhappy life by tremulously believing in the good, the beautiful, and the true.

When Frost had children of his own, he told them the same Bible stories, he celebrated Christmas, and he taught for a time at Pinkerton Academy, a Congregational school. But he was at no time a firm member of any Christian sect; and in the nineties he shocked his mother by saying he was a free-thinker. This was partly adolescent brag and partly truth. It is perhaps significant that in *North of Boston*, though there are farmhouses and hotels, there are no churches; and that the only minister is the loquacious clergyman of no particular denomination who tells us about the old lady of the black cottage. The minister speaks this famous passage:

> . . . dear me, why abandon a belief
> Merely because it ceases to be true.
> Cling to one long enough, and not a doubt
> It will turn true again, for so it goes.
> Most of the change we think we see in life
> Is due to truths being in and out of favor.

This may be good William James theorizing about the will to believe, but it is not very good theology. I may add that Frost's long poem about New Hampshire says nothing whatever about churches in that state.

There was a streak of desperation in the Frost inheritance, sadly evinced by the cases of insanity and suicide in the family and evidenced also by the poet's struggle to overcome depressive and suicidal components in his own makeup. The movement away from Christianity toward some other form of belief therefore took on for him a harried and immediate urgency. Whatever Christian faith he may have known was deeply disturbed as with others of his generation by reading such movers and shakers as Darwin, Huxley, Spencer, Henry Drummond (author of *Natural Law in the Spiritual World*), and, above all, Richard A. Proctor, who published an attractive popular book on astronomy, *Our Place Among the Infinities*. I lay emphasis upon Proctor because of the important place night and astronomy hold in Frost's poetry. During his dark years at Derry, New Hampshire—since the days of Bronson Alcott New England had seldom seen a more impractical farmer—he read Emerson and Thoreau; by and by, at Harvard, he was impressed by the thought of William James and put off by the philosophy—or was it the classroom manner?—of George Santayana. He later discovered Bergson's *Creative Evolution*, traces of which are to be found throughout his mature poetry. Among the ironies of the Frost story is that his first poem was sold to *The Independent*, a Christian magazine edited by the Rev. William Hayes Ward; and when Frost, full of enthusiasm for Bergson, went to see Ward and tried to persuade him that Bergson was a distinguished spiritual philosopher, he was coldly informed that Bergson was an atheist. This bleak exposure to theological intolerance seems to have driven Frost even farther away from Christianity.

II

If one could read Frost's poetry with an entirely fresh eye, something impossible to most of us, I think one would be impressed, among other characteristics, by a negative one—a curious and virtually conscious antisocial quality. Not for Frost Whitman's dear love of comrades. Not for him any utterance comparable to the older poet's

> One's-self I sing, a simple, separate person,
> Yet utter the word Democratic, the word En-Masse.

Frost is not merely the poet of the farm and the village, the cel-
lar-hole and the road that goes nowhere; he expresses an active
hostility to metropolitan life. This aversion to the city poignant-
ly appears in one of his best poems, "Acquainted with the
Night":

> I have been one acquainted with the night.
> I have walked out in rain—and back in rain.
> I have outwalked the furthest city light.
>
> I have looked down the saddest city lane.
> I have passed by the watchman on his beat
> And dropped my eyes, unwilling to explain.
>
> I have stood still and stopped the sound of feet
> When far away an interrupted cry
> Came over houses from another street,
>
> But not to call me back or say good-by;
> And further still at an unearthly height,
> One luminary clock against the sky
>
> Proclaimed the time was neither wrong nor right.
> I have been one acquainted with the night.

It will be remarked that not only is the solitary walker silhouet-
ted against the night, but also that the components of the city
image here are all unsympathetic—the saddest lane, the watch-
man on his beat, an interrupted cry over houses from another
street, the unearthly luminary clock. The solitary walker in the
rain is not merely solitary, he also takes some satisfaction in
being, or having been, beyond the furthest city light. No poet is
under any obligation to be sociological, but it is important to
notice that for Frost the city is an artificial thing apart from, and
other than, nature.

But the solitariness of Frost goes beyond a dislike of the city.
There are poems for or about children in his work, and they are
charming, but they are so rare as to be negligible. There are no

poems of friendship, the theme that stirred Tennyson to *In Memoriam* and Arnold to *Thyrsis*, though there are books dedicated to friends. Like any other poet he writes love poems, sometimes shyly concealing ardor under an intricate image or symbol. Misunderstandings are a constant theme in poems about love, but the misunderstandings between lovers in Robert Frost seem to go beyond lovers' tiffs and are produced by some deep solitariness, some unbreakable barrier between soul and soul. The loving are not less the lonely. One of these poems is unique.

This is "The Subverted Flower," Frost's solitary poem of physical passion, and it is enigmatic. In this story the male lashes his palm with a flower, assumes that the girl is sexually stirred, but succeeds only in frightening her into motionlessness

> Lest movement should provoke
> The demon of pursuit
> That slumbers in a brute.

The girl understands neither the symbolism of the flower nor the healthy lust in the man and spits bitter words at him till he stumbles away. Her mother calls. The girl is turned into a wild animal by the sexual threat, and

> Her mother wiped the foam
> From her chin, picked up her comb
> And drew her backward home.

"The Subverted Flower" may be construed in various ways, but one has only to murmur something about Browning's

> O lyric love, half angel and half bird
> And all a wonder and a wild desire

to discover the distance between this poem and what used to be called romance.

In his journey from the lyricism of *A Boy's Will* through the

dramatic narratives of *North of Boston* to the gnomic and philosophical verse of his later volumes Frost either isolates the individual or treats mankind facelessly and in the mass as nation or
race. Poem after poem shows the speaker or the person drama-
tized running off or living alone. In Chaucer you are advised to
flee from the press and dwell with steadfastness, but in Robert
Frost he who flees goes to confront the vast enigma of space and
the night. Frost can occasionally be funny on this subject:

> But outer Space,
> At least this far,
> For all the fuss
> Of the populace,
> Stays more popular
> Than populous,

but his clowning does not conceal a genuine contempt for popular judgment. On earth

> You linger your little hour and are gone,
> And still the woods sweep leafily on,
> Not even missing the coral-root flower
> You took as a trophy of the hour.

And as for the universe,

> We dance round in a ring and suppose,
> But the Secret sits in the middle and knows.

I shall return to this theme in a moment.

In Frost's earlier poems, with of course large exceptions, men
in the more natural environment—farmers, villagers, tramps,
woodsmen, hunters, and so on—are likelier to lead a healthy and
interesting existence than men in cities. But one of the large exceptions is women. Not all the women in Frost are oddities, but
the memorable female figures all exhibit some streak of singular-
ity. If loneliness may be bracing for the male, for the female it is

more likely to be disastrous. She will bear loneliness out of love
for a time (sometimes not even then), but when love falters or
fails, the woman is not infrequently lost in the woods or broken
down into madness. Familiar instances are poems like "Home
Burial," "A Servant to Servants," "The Fear," and "The Hill
Wife." Man successfully confronting nature in Frost is principally the male animal.

III

What nature does man confront? Nature in the first instance
is simply the earthly environment of man in the temperate zone
—Frost never writes about the tropics and seldom about the
Arctic. The theme of nature as cosmic vastness, which occupies
much space in his later books, appears only casually in *Mountain
Interval* (1916) and does not become a major topic until his
sixth book, *A Further Range* (1936), where it has helped create
the title. Yet nature taken only as New England landscape is
from the beginning ambiguous. It both comforts and threatens.
Its cycles can be trusted as the process of nature in Lucretius
can be trusted, but its disasters are eerie and unpredictable. It is
the mother and home of man and it is simultaneously utterly
indifferent to him.

This ambiguity is already apparent in *A Boy's Will*, as three
poems from the early collection will testify. In "The Vantage
Point" the poet announces he is tired of trees and wants to seek
out mankind. The seeking out is typically Frostian, for he climbs
a hill and spends the morning looking at distant white houses
and a graveyard. By noon he is weary, turns on his arm, smells
the earth, smells the bruised plant, and looks into the crater of
the ant, the implication being, I take it, that man's spirit is
soothed by an experience that emphasizes at once his superiority

to, and his fusion with, natural process. A second poem is called "In Hardwood Groves" and meditates on the fall of the leaf; only as the leaves fall, decay, and enrich the soil, can the spring flowers be born, and the poem concludes:

> However it is in some other world
> I know that this is the way in ours.

The third poem, a key utterance which follows upon a rather conventional bit of verse about Pan, is "The Demiurge's Laugh." In this the poet, hunting after secret nature, suddenly hears a sound behind him that he shall never forget:

> The sound was behind me instead of before,
>   A sleepy sound, but mocking half,
> As of one who utterly couldn't care.
>   The Demon arose from his wallow to laugh,
> Brushing the dirt from his eye as he went;
> And well I knew what the Demon meant.

> I shall not forget how his laugh rang out,
>   I felt as a fool to have been so caught,
> And checked my steps to make pretense
>   It was something among the leaves I sought
> (Though doubtful whether he stayed to see).
> Thereafter I sat me against a tree.

Sitting against a tree is, as it were, symbolic; the poet comes to realize more and more this law of nature: thus far shall you go and no farther. Frost cannot agree with Wordsworth that nature never did betray the heart that loved her.

As the years went by, as his personal sorrows accumulated around him and the poet came to be more and more aware of the pretentiousness of all human theorizing, Frost was more and more shaken by the ambiguous place of man in nature. In one poem a human couple in the woods suddenly and silently confront a doe and a buck, and it seems to them for a moment that earth returns their love. But in a late poem, "The Most of It," the speaker, thinking to get an answer from the universe and receiving nothing but the echo of his own voice, finally hears another sound—a great buck swims a lake and stumbles over the rocks with heavy tread, and that is all. If in "West-running Brook" the backward-sloping wave can be interpreted as man's partial control of nature, this is followed almost immediately by two poems, "The Last Mowing" and "The Birthplace," pictures of abandoned farms where

> The mountain pushed us off her knees.
> And now her lap is full of trees.

Late poems have much to say about the helplessness of man in the face of natural catastrophes, and one poem, of extreme ghastliness, directed against the teleological argument and ironically called "Design," pictures a fat white spider holding up a white moth on a white flower called heal-all, concluding:

> What had that flower to do with being white,
> The wayside blue and innocent heal-all?
> What brought the kindred spider to that height,
> Then steered the white moth thither in the night?
> What but design of darkness to appall?—
> If design govern in a thing so small.

I think Frost's pessimism increased with the years, but so far as man's relation to the immediacy of earth is concerned I think also that his central tenet, whatever contradictions may appear, is what I may call a pessimistic but bracing stoicism, a humanistic faith not found in Mark Twain, that whatever the odds against him, man the indestructible must not confuse his doubts about the earth with a total distrust of nature. After all, a good many infallible theories have risen and died in history. A poem "On a Tree Fallen Across the Road" makes the tree an emblem of nature's dropping it just to make us ask us who we think we are. But nature

> knows obstruction is in vain:
> We will not be put off the final goal
> We have it hidden in us to attain,
> Not though we have to seize earth by the pole
>
> And, tired of aimless circling in one place,
> Steer straight off after something into space.

But what is that something? In a poem entitled "For Once, Then, Something," responding to the taunt that if truth lie at the bottom of a well, he, Robert Frost, has never got beyond the solipsism of making earth refract himself, the poet says that, looking over the well-curb into a well, he once thought he saw something beyond and beneath the reflection of his own face— something white but uncertain. But

> Water came to rebuke the too clear water

as a drop fell from a fern and made a ripple that blurred or blotted out whatever lay at the bottom.

> What was that whiteness?
> Truth? A pebble of quartz? For once, then, something.

This fleeting vision was no stay against confusion; and I suppose that the best single statement of what seems to be Frost's humanism—that is, his assumption that there is somehow a regulative relationship between mankind and nature in her normal moods—has something again to do with water.

There is a very fine poem, "Directive," which appeared in the collection called *Steeple Bush*, in 1947. In this poem the seeker goes to a lost farm this side of a mountain. On the way there the journeyer is watched by eyes from forty cellar-holes—one's mind goes back to "The Demiurge's Laugh"—but finally reaches the site of the abandoned farm, where there are still some shattered children's toys. The "destination," the "destiny" of the speaker, is not the spot where once the house stood, nor the toys, but rather a brook that was once the water of the house, a brook always untouched by floods. Near it some one has hidden a broken drinking goblet

> like the Grail
> Under a spell so the wrong ones can't find it,

and the seeker is directed to take up the glass,

> Drink and be whole again beyond confusion.

This seems to mean that man can be whole and sane if he will only accept nature as an entity that is sane; that is, not mistake catastrophe, death, and disappearance for the main intent of the natural order of which man is a part—so much a part that when he tries to build artificial cities and live a life that is not in this sense natural, he becomes not merely unnatural but essentially inhumane. Such a doctrine, it must be confessed, is for city-dwellers a humanism hard to come by.

IV

So far I have spoken only of the earth as the setting of the human predicament. But Frost is also a poet of the universe, especially in his later volumes. A Christian interpretation of the universe interested him so little that he virtually ignores it. "Trial by Existence" in A Boy's Will seems, to be sure, to imply some sort of personal immortality, but it is a concept of immortality that owes more to Swedenborg and Browning than it owes to the Bible. The point of this early poem seems to be that the brave on earth will be required to be brave hereafter and not

relax; and also that, in some previous existence, they had chosen
to be brave and to suffer on earth:

> 'Tis of the essence of life here,
> Though we choose greatly, still to lack
> The lasting memory at all clear,
> That life has had for us on the wrack
> Nothing but what we somehow chose.

This, however, is more like the transmigration of souls in Oriental thought than it is like Christian theology; and I think it
interesting to note that for a collection of Frost's poems called
Aforesaid, published to celebrate his eightieth birthday, Frost
wrote in a preface that in his vaguely Christian youth, he mis-
read Emerson's "Brahma," taking the line

> But thou, meek lover of the good,

to refer to Christ. Fifty years later he reads the poem more wise-
ly. Meekness means a perfect detachment from ambition and
desire, and the "me" of the poem worth turning "thy back on
Heaven" for is Nirvana, "the only nothing that is something."

I have earlier remarked that Frost was a great lover of the
night. I add that astronomy was a lifelong passion with him, and
that, though he did not read profoundly in modern scientific
theory, his annual progress among the universities led to his
picking up a great deal of information about modern physical
and astronomical theory. Where other poets have been shaped
by philosophical theory, Frost has been influenced by scientific
speculation. I turn therefore from earth as man's natural setting
to the vast problem of man on earth confronting the total universe.

Discussing Thomas Hardy, one critic has remarked that there
is a size at which greatness begins, a size at which grandeur
begins, and a size at which ghastliness begins. The contemporary

universe seems to many sensitive souls to have reached the size of ghastliness. Doubtless from the intellectual point of view infinity has not changed since Pascal suspended man on a tiny point between two abysses, but the gigantic expansion of the universe in space-time, the problem of the relation of mass to energy, and the puzzle whether the universe is expanding indefinitely or pulsating in an expansion-contraction rhythm too enormous to comprehend, have altered the impact of the universe on modern minds. Today the solar system is not even the inconsiderable speck of Frost's amusing poem; and the gigantism of Mark Twain's imagination, which still postulated a heaven, God, Satan, and the other archangels, looks comfortable and cozy in comparison with ours. Many poets refuse to look into the abyss; others are alternately fascinated and repelled by the dimension of ghastliness. Frost's attitude seems to be of this *odi et amo* kind. He wants to turn away and content himself with the human condition, but he is compelled willy-nilly to consider the universal dark.

One can begin with some poems in the volume called *New Hampshire* of 1926, wherein this *odi et amo* point of view begins to emerge. In "The Star-Splitter" we read of a farmer who burns down his farmhouse, collects the insurance, and buys a telescope because, as he says,

> The best thing that we're put here for's to see.

But the telescope is imperfect, splitting every star into two or three; and the narrator's comment is:

> We've looked and looked, but after all where are we?
> Do we know any better where we are,
> And how it stands between the night to-night
> And a man with a smoky lantern chimney?
> How different from the way it ever stood?

Here the universe is incomprehensible. In "I Will Sing You One-O" in the same volume the poet, unable to go to sleep, hears several clocks strike one, whereupon his imagination goes careening off beyond the farthest constellations. The peal of the clocks speaks bravely for the clock of the universe, a universe so immense even distant exploding stars seem stationary to us. This inhuman machine has not changed to the eye since man began to drag down man and nation to drag down nation. Here the universe is indifferent. In a third poem, "Misgiving," the leaves of trees, that all summer had seemed to want to go with the wind, now that autumn comes and they are free to be blown, gather instead in hollows and back of walls, and the poet's comment is:

> I only hope that when I am free
> As they are free to go in quest
> Of the knowledge beyond the bounds of life
> It may not seem better to me to rest.

In West-Running Brook, published in 1928, the poet turns his back resolutely upon outer space and stands firmly on this planet, since no anticipated cosmic catastrophe ever occurs:

> We may as well go patiently on with our life,
> And look elsewhere than to stars and moon and sun
> For the shocks and changes we need to keep us sane.
>
> Still it wouldn't reward the watcher to stay awake
> In hopes of seeing the calm of heaven break
> On his particular time and personal sight.
> That calm seems certainly safe to last tonight.

But in the next volume, A Further Range (1936), another poem urges precisely the opposite point of view. It is called "Lost in Heaven":

The clouds, the source of rain, one stormy night
Offered an opening to the source of dew;
Which I accepted with impatient sight,
Looking for my old skymarks in the blue.

But stars were scarce in that part of the sky,
And no two were of the same constellation—
No one was bright enough to identify;
So 'twas with not ungrateful consternation,

Seeing myself well lost once more, I sighed,
"Where, where in Heaven am I? But don't tell me!"
I warned the clouds, "by opening on me wide.
Let's let my heavenly lostness overwhelm me."

The astronomical theme looms largest in the three late volumes of collected poems, *A Witness Tree* (1942), *Steeple Bush* (1947), and *In the Clearing* (1962), always with the same ambiguity of resolution. In that amazing address to a poet of the time of Charlemagne called "The Lesson for Today'" about whether the ninth or the twentieth century is gloomier, Frost puts the problem boldly:

Space ails us moderns: we are sick with space.
Its contemplation makes us out as small
As a brief epidemic of microbes
That in a good glass may be seen to crawl
The patina of this the least of globes.
But have we there the advantage after all?
You were belittled into vilest worms
God hardly tolerated with his feet;
Which comes to the same thing in different terms.
We both are the belittled human race,
One as compared with God and one with space.
I had thought ours the more profound disgrace;
But doubtless this was only my conceit.
The cloister and the observatory saint
Take comfort in about the same complaint.
So science and religion really meet.

The conclusion is:

> There is a limit to our time extension.
> We all are doomed to broken-off careers,
> And so's the nation, so's the total race.
> The earth itself is liable to the fate
> Of meaninglessly being broken off.

For religion, in "Innate Helium," a poem in *Steeple Bush*, we find this curiously ambiguous metaphor:

> Religious faith is a most filling vapor.
> It swirls occluded in us under tight
> Compression to uplift us out of weight—
> As in those buoyant bird bones thin as paper,
> To give them still more buoyancy in flight.
> Some gas like helium must be innate.

But science, in another poem in the same book, comes out somewhat peculiarly also:

> Sarcastic Science she would like to know,
> In her complacent ministry of fear,
> How we propose to get away from here
> When she has made things so we have to go
> Or be wiped out. Will she be asked to show
> Us how by rocket we may hope to steer
> To some star off there say a half light-year
> Through temperatures of absolute zeró?
> Why wait for Science to supply the how
> When any amateur can tell it now?
> The way to go away should be the same
> As fifty million years ago we came—
> If anyone remembers how that was.
> I have a theory, but it hardly does.

Is this enigmatic statement about a concealed theory that won't somehow do, Frost's final confession of faith as he confronts the outer dark? I do not know, nor perhaps did he, but remembering

with him that the heart should not cloud the mind, I cite the
final quatrain of a poem in *A Further Range:*

> Wind goes from farm to farm in wave on wave,
> But carries no cry of what is hoped to be.
> There may be little or much beyond the grave,
> The strong are saying nothing until they see.

This idea is extended to outer space in *In the Clearing:*

> Don't think I leave
> For the outer dark
> Like Adam and Eve
> Put out of the Park.
>
> Forget the myth.
> There is no one I
> Am put out with
> Or put out by.

V

But what about God?

Virtually the only poem in the works of Robert Frost that
assumes Christian theology is the nameless dedicatory poem to
In the Clearing. In this the Incarnation is regarded as proof that
spirit enters flesh, charging into earth in birth after birth, but
the poem's ending is scarcely sound theology, however it might
have delighted Emerson:

> We may take the view
> That its derring-do
> Thought of in the large
> Is one mighty charge
> On our human part
> Of the soul's ethereal
> Into the material.

So far as God the Creator is concerned, one poem in this same
volume, "Accidentally on Purpose," seems to take the point of

view that the universe was self-created, that it accidentally hit on mind, and that man is the purpose of creation. Frost, however, comments that it—that is, the universe—must have had the purpose from the first to produce purpose in man, who is "just purpose coming to a head."

> Whose purpose was it? His or Hers or Its?
> Let's leave that to the scientific wits.
> Grant me intention, purpose, and design—
> That's near enough for me to the Divine.

The poem does not indicate whether or not the design was self-established. In other poems the name of God is a mere convention. In A *Further Range* we read:

> I turned to speak to God
> About the world's despair;
> But to make bad matters worse
> I found God wasn't there.
>
> God turned to speak to me
> (Don't anybody laugh)
> God found I wasn't there—
> At least not over half.

In another poem God is the Lord of Seven Heavens, and Frost asks only that he be taken to one of them, since he is entitled to go up, not down. In a letter to Louis Untermeyer written in 1928 he said that the logic of everything lands you outside of it, so that

the logic of religion by nice gradations [leads you] outside of Catholicism in Protestantism, outside of Protestantism in agnosticism, and finally outside of agnosticism in Watsonian behaviorism. . . . Life is a fight we say and deify the prize fighter. We could go further and say life is a night-club and its presiding deity a *retired* prizefighter or Bouncer, bouncing us forever out.[1]

[1] *The Letters of Robert Frost to Louis Untermeyer* (New York, 1963), p. 188.

And a poem in *Steeple Bush*, "The Fear of God," turns on no Christian conception:

> If you should rise from Nowhere up to Somewhere,
> From being No One up to being Someone,
> Be sure to keep repeating to yourself
> You owe it to an arbitrary god
> Whose mercy to you rather than to others
> Won't bear too critical examination.
> Stay unassuming. If for lack of license
> To wear the uniform of who you are,
> You should be tempted to make up for it
> In a subordinating look or tone
> Beware of coming too much to the surface,
> And using for apparel what was meant
> To be the curtain of the inmost soul.

At first, in reading this poem, one is tempted to murmur something about the doctrine of election, but I think what we have is rather the ancient fear of the gods that is one of the oldest components of religious history. I remarked earlier that Frost insists upon human loneliness; surely this late poem paints the loneliness of the soul rather than any dependence on deity. God exists, and Frost says many things about the assumption that He does so. Were I to characterize his notion of God, I would reply that the God of Frost lies somewhere between the God of Job and the God of Voltaire. My reason for saying this is that in Frost's two masques about reason and justice God is neither the stern and majestic Yahve of the Book of Job nor the logician of Voltaire's universe. If God is the Person of Persons of some systems of theology, God in *A Masque of Reason* appears as a somewhat bumbling and kindly old gentleman who needs the help of man. It can also be said that Frost becomes virtually a Manichaean in these little plays, wherein the forces of good and evil are from eternity and shall not fail.

The masques have, I supposed, irritated or puzzled as many readers as they have pleased. *A Masque of Reason* (1943) is a commentary on the Book of Job; *A Masque of Mercy* (1947), a modern extension of the story of Jonah. *A Masque of Mercy* is the weaker of the two. In the first place the Book of Jonah is itself far from impressive, and since what most of us remember of the Jonah story is Jonah's being swallowed by a great fish, it is unsatisfactory to have the little play staged in a New York bookshop. In the second place hell is somewhat imperfectly represented by the cellar beneath the shop. In the third place the characters in *A Masque of Mercy* are assembled, they do not come out of the original story, which, after all, concerns only God and Jonah as *dramatis personae*, and in the masque God does not appear. The dialog is carried on by the Apostle Paul and Jezebel in modern guise, and the nameless keeper of the shop, originally christened My Brother's Keeper, which I find a little hard to take. Finally, the problem of justice versus mercy is by no means illuminated through the death of Jonah just before the curtain falls. The philosophic point, however, is clear. The Keeper says:

> But I'm too much afraid of God to claim
> I have been fighting on the angels' side.
> And I can see that the uncertainty
> In which we act is a severity,
> A cruelty, amounting to injustice
> That nothing but God's mercy can assuage.
> Nothing can make injustice just but mercy.

This is fair enough, but it is a little difficult to see how this conclusion follows from the action of the play.

A Masque of Reason is better work. The characters are all from the Book of Job; and in place of writing a modern version of that majestic theme, Frost was content to put down a retro-

spective commentary in modern terms. Both masques avail
themselves of the Aristophanic privilege of being disrespectful to
the gods, and the waggishness of *A Masque of Reason* is here
and there a little out of key, but the poem drives straight to its
point. Years have gone by. Job and his wife are seen under a
palm tree in an oasis. God appears, bringing with him a portable
plywood throne. He comes to thank Job for having helped Him
to

> Establish once for all the principle
> There's no connection man can reason out
> Between his just deserts and what he gets.

"My thanks are to you," He says, for releasing Me

> From moral bondage to the human race.
> The only free will there at first was man's,
> Who could do good or evil as he chose.
> I had no choice but I must follow him
> With forfeits and rewards he understood—
> Unless I liked to suffer loss of worship.
> I had to prosper good and punish evil.
> You changed all that.

When Job and his wife continue to press Him, God says:

> The tempter comes to me and I am tempted.
> I'd had about enough of his derision
> Of what I valued most in human nature.
> He thinks he's smart. He thinks he can convince me
> It is no different with my followers
> From what it is with his. . . .
>   He could count on no one:
> That was his look out. I could count on you.
>   I took your side
> Against your comforters in their contention
> You must be wicked to deserve such pain.

Once again, it seems to me, the note of heroic loneliness is
sounded.

Such, then, as I read him, is the world-view of Robert Frost, beneath the plain surface of whose poems there lurks what somebody once called the most mischievous mind in America. One can find as many interpretations of Frost as there are commentators, and I am by no means certain I am correct in my reading of him. Yet it appears that in Frost God is either a human construct or a being so remote from man as to be meaningless. The universe is indifferent to man's fate, though the poet nourishes a secret hope that astronomical vastness and the inconceivability of atomic energy only conceal some cryptic future for the soul of man. Meanwhile we are on this planet, where it does no good to complain of cruelty and catastrophe. The process of nature is, up to a point, predictable; to substitute a gloomy view of natural catastrophes for a plain reading of the seasonal cycle, to substitute accident, however overwhelming, for normal behavior is a misreading of earth. We are here; and we may expect to be here as a race for a very long time. It is idle to berate the Old Testament God as Thomas Paine did, wrong to ignore accident and disaster and emphasize a smooth-running teleology as Cooper and Bryant did, wrong also to assume that there is an Over-Soul that happily communicates with us, or a mysterious spiritual entity peculiar to man that Whitman calls the dear love of comrades. Nor is Frost impressed by the Sunday-school universe of Mark Twain, a universe blown up to enormous dimensions and very colorful. Frost is nearer the British poet, A. E. Housman, but whereas Housman exhorts men to endure, Frost, discontent with a stoic passiveness, does not deny to man the possibility that the mere fact of his perpetual craving may create the object he craves. I think his final view appears in a poem in *In the Clearing* entitled "Escapist—Never," a poem by no means easy to read. But here it is:

He is no fugitive—escaped, escaping.
No one has seen him stumble looking back.
His fear is not behind him but beside him
On either hand to make his course perhaps
A crooked straightness yet no less a straightness.
He runs face forward. He is a pursuer.
He seeks a seeker who in his turn seeks
Another still, lost far into the distance.
Any who seek him seek in him the seeker.
His life is a pursuit of a pursuit forever.
It is the future that creates his present.
All is an interminable chain of longing.

This is a difficult statement. Its modern meaning is, I think, made clearer if we ponder over Frost's magnificent sonnet, "A Soldier," from West-Running Brook, a poem that seems to me not only to sum up the pathos and the majesty of any war but also to fuse into a single vision the apparently contradictory elements of volition and determinism, integrity and helplessness, that are for this poet the riddle of mankind upon this painful earth:

He is that fallen lance that lies as hurled,
That lies unlifted now, come dew, come rust,
But still lies pointed as it plowed the dust.
If we who sight along it round the world,
See nothing worthy to have been its mark,
It is because like men we look too near,
Forgetting that as fitted to the sphere,
Our missiles always make too short an arc.
They fall, they rip the grass, they intersect
The curve of earth, and striking, break their own;
They make us cringe for metal-point on stone.
But this we know, the obstacle that checked
And tripped the body, shot the spirit on
Further than target ever showed or shone.

The scientific figure, the accuracy of the metaphor about metal-point on stone, the sense of the high idealism and the ignoble fact of war, the truth that man is trapped within the curve of earth—all this does not affect a secret and stubborn idealism in Robert Frost, who hints that spirit may be shot forward to some distant goal further than target ever showed or shone.[2]

[2] This poem, allegorically taken, and a parenthetical expression in Frost's introduction to an edition of *King Jasper* by Edwin Arlington Robinson (New York, 1935) saying that "Religion is merely consolation for what we don't know"—a characteristic bit of irony—is about as far as Frost gets to "defining" religion.

POSTLUDE

THE PATTERN of the annual lectures under the auspices of the Frank L. Weil Institute for Studies in Religion and the Humanities is that there shall be six addresses on an appropriate theme given before a general audience seriously interested in the relations between the two great phases of life specified in the title of the Institute. The virtue of limiting the number of lectures is obvious, and the advantage of addressing a general audience is that it prevents the speaker from taking refuge in technical language and forces him to present a scholarly theme in simpler terms. But these virtues have an inevitable accompanying defect. The lecturer must be conscious, and the specialist may become so, of the danger of sweeping over complicated puzzles with facile generalizations.

As my introductory lecture indicates, I sought to simplify a complex historical problem by confining myself to American authors writing during the decades of our independence, and paying only enough attention to the colonial period to set the stage. I chose six authors or groups of authors who seemed to me to represent important phases of the relation between belief and literature. Other choices are quite possible. One could, for example, set up the sequence: John Adams, Herman Melville, Edgar

Allan Poe, Henry James, Henry Adams, and William Faulkner, and come out with a different set of analyses.

But though other names could be substituted for my list, I doubt that any other list of major names from 1776 to 1966 would develop a fundamental shift toward some sort of alliance between religious dogma and literary art. There are of course in the nineteenth century and in this one some "Christian" authors, just as there are Jewish authors. But if one accepts the general canon of our literary classics, together with more recent books judged to be important in imaginative literature by the critics, I do not see that the direct presentation of any system of religious orthodoxy has at any time been a matter of major concern to most major American writers. There are, I am sure, exceptions, but the general rule seems to hold.

Does this mean that the alliance between religion and poetry that produced the *Aeneid* in ancient times and the *Divine Comedy* in the late Middle Ages has no force in American writing? There is no simple answer. We have had American plays about saints and martyrs, but these have always a historical air. For Dante politics, philosophy, history, and theology were parts of one great, universal whole; and I think that for Americans, even for devout Americans of any persuasion, this simplicity is impossible because the unity of knowledge that sustained it has disappeared. It is not merely, as I have said earlier, that our literary tradition has been overwhelmingly Protestant and individualistic. The fundamental difficulty is that the world order of Newton or in its turn the world order of Einstein is several light years away from the Ptolemaic world order that sustains the *Divine Comedy*.

Moreover, since the beginning of the nineteenth century and particularly since the Civil War the influence and authority of minister, priest, and rabbi have declined and the authority of the scientist and the social scientist (and latterly of the psychologist) has steadily advanced. Neither writers nor readers now take the voice of any church as the utterer of everlasting truth in any major department of art. We do not patiently suffer censorship, and the American pragmatic spirit makes us as readers suspicious of any sort of dogma concealed in literature that has too palpable a design upon us. It is true, of course, that "inspirational" books sell by the thousands of copies. But I am speaking of serious literary art.

I have said that there are probably exceptions, and the vogue of T. S. Eliot can be cited. Mr. Eliot during his life had a commanding position as a poet, a critic, and a moralist. But I think it significant that shortly after publishing *The Waste-Land* he went to England, where they manage things differently. It does not appear that he has been succeeded in this country by any American of like stature and similar views. Much that looks like religious coloring in serious American writing is ambiguous, the ambiguity arising from our confusion of guilt in the psychiatric sense and sin in the Christian sense. "Guilt" may indeed be "purged," but the purgation is supposed to be evidenced by a well-adjusted secular career.

Whatever the merit in these speculations, it is evident that the classic American writers and the standard modern ones, if they are not "religious," are not therefore atheists. It is still true of serious writing that the great themes of literature are in a sense the great themes of religion. The existence and nature of God, His interest in man and the universe if He has any, the riddle of the purpose and rationale of the universe, and the grave question whether man is more than an animal—these themes are the themes of literature, ancient, medieval, and modern. It may rest on a platitude (but I have a great respect for platitudes) if I remark that sentimental poetry by Longfellow about maidenhood and *The Children's Hour* by Lillian Hellman, Whittier's barefoot boy and the unloved and unlovely Holden Caulfield of *Catcher in the Rye* are alike in this: their creators assume that the young human animal, male or female, should be more than a young animal.

What is forever at stake in serious literature is the nature of humanity itself, that glory, jest, and riddle of the world. No slightest trace of theology, I think, went to the making of *Herzog* by Saul Bellow, but *Herzog* has this in common with *Pilgrim's Progress*, that its central issue is the problem of salvation. God may be dead, whatever the phrase means, and the secular city may come to prevail over the sanctuary, but writers continue to be imaginatively entangled in—I think the modern word is "identify"—the problems of fate, foreknowledge, and free will that exercised the ingenious wits of Milton's fallen angels while they waited Satan's return from a scouting expedition against Eden. A good many books about American culture bewail the fall of the American Adam and the loss of Eden without offering any hope that one greater man shall restore us and regain the blissful seat. But if Adam and Eden mean so little, why do not these critics rejoice over getting rid of such rubbish? On the contrary, they lament: *tempora pessima, hora novissima!*

These lectures chronicle the almost continuous failure of religious orthodoxy in America to appeal to the serious literary imagination. They do not chronicle the refusal of the authors I have discussed to express a grave concern about the problem of belief in the life of their times. The truth is that no author worth his salt fails to grapple with one or more of the three great themes of theology—God, man, and the universe. As literary scholarship and literary criticism incline too often to take a short-range view of the nature of literature, these lectures will have succeeded if they remind the reader that art cannot long absent itself from the central problems of human existence. Tom Paine furiously assailed the Bible because it contained the myth of Eden and the fall of man; the modern critic, less religious than Paine, laments the loss of Eden and the failure of innocence. But they are both talking (or writing) about much the same thing. There are religions without a literature; I cannot think of a literature with no religion, not even in Russia—and by this I do not mean writing patterned on a creed but only writing answering an ancient appeal: What is Man? As William Faulkner said in his Nobel Prize Address, in the long run man will prevail. However despicable the unlovely characters in many modern novels may be, the authors wrestle desperately with the ancient problem of the differentiating quality that separates human nature from animal nature. Late nineteenth-century realism was satisfied, or thought it was, to trace the operations of scientific law, usually biological, on the human animal; modern writers find this too naïve and struggle to disentangle the eternal nature of humanity from the dark unconscious drives of Freud, Jung, and other secular psychological saints. But is not all this to try to answer the ancient question, "What is man that Thou art mindful of him?" Imaginative American writing has more or less turned its back upon the church and upon theology; it has not turned its back upon the necessity of belief of some sort in man as man.

INDEX

NOTE: Since this book discusses at large such concepts as religious belief, God, immortality, and the soul, the index is limited to specific religious sects and movements. It also omits the names of persons referred to casually that do not necessarily appertain to a particular set of ideas, theology, or like leading concepts.